THE GUIDE
TO THE ARCHAEOLOGICAL SITE

POMPEII

Everyday life in the town buried
by Mount Vesuvius 2000 years ago

MARIUS
Edizioni - POMPEI

- 2002 -

POMPEII
THE TOWN ON THE SEA

THE FOUNDING OF THE TOWN

Pompeii was originally situated on the coast at the centre of the Gulf of Naples, a fact that could be the key to understanding the birth of Italy's most admired archaeological site. There is evidence of settlements dating as far back as the early 9th century B.C., but these were only found in the inland areas of the Sarno valley while there were none on the coast.

The only hill in the area was located at the mouth of the river Sarno in a strategic position in the centre of the Gulf of Naples and at the intersection of the main roads. The river mouth was thus a natural outlet for trade while the hillside served as a natural rampart to defend the area's inhabitants and the fertile farms situated inland. For these reasons the resident Italic peoples chose it as an ideal site for a settlement.

The Temple of Apollo

*The Triangular Forum
was a type of acropolis.*

The first Oscan buildings sprung up here and there in positions dictated primarily by the geography of the hillside on a site behind the current Forum. The settlement covered an area of about 10 hectares (approx. 25 acres) that extended eastwards to the valley in which the Via Stabiana was later built.

In Pompeii we find the remains of settlements established throughout the following two centuries, especially during the 6th century B.C., when the originally Oscan towns of Stabiae and Nuceria grew under Etruscan influence. Moreover there are certain elements that suggest there were economic and cultural links between the various settlements in the area.

As can be seen from the remains of the old town wall, built of blocks of dark grey tuff stone called 'Pappa-

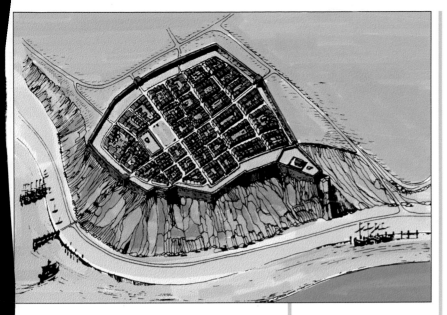

monte', an area of approximately 66 hectares (about 163 acres), representing nearly the whole surface area occupied by the present-day town, was protected by defensive structures. There then followed a period of sparse residential development, with small groups of houses built at roadsides and large areas designated for vegetable and ornamental gardens. The Etruscan community evidently intended to stay in this area, as is shown by findings of a temple under the Temple of Apollo, in the neighbouring districts, in the Stabian Baths, in the Triangular Forum and in various other parts of the town.

The Etruscans had already laid deep cultural and economic roots in the Gulf of Naples, and Pompeii provided an ideal location for a settlement in terms of trade and defence as it had a safe harbour for warships and a port for loading and unloading trading vessels.

The influence of the Etruscans lasted until the middle of the 5th century B.C. when their fleet suffered heavy losses at the hands of the Greeks from Syracuse in the waters of Cumae, marking the end of the first phase of the town's life.

Archaeologists have found no votive offerings from this period in **the temple of Apollo** - a sure sign that the community had effectively disintegrated, only to reestablish itself again under the influence of the Greeks from nearby Neapolis. The following period is not well-documented, but the town certainly fell under the influence of the Samnites, a people from the mountains of Irpinia and Sannio in the Appennine regions of Campania.

The fact that there are no records documenting the history of Pompeii between the 5th and 1st centuries B.C. suggests that the area was not of any great political importance at that time.

In the absence of documentary records, the only archaeological research that can be carried out is through the investigation of the building works performed in and around the town.

By studying the town, wall archaeologists have acquired precious information on the history of

Vicolo dei Soprastanti, Via degli Augustali, Via del Lupanare and Via dei Teatri mark out the boundaries of the so-called 'Old Town'.

Via Stabiana.

Pompeii under the assumption that all new works on the defensive wall coincided with periods in which the town was under threat from enemy raids. The original wall of soft 'Pappamonte' stone was later reinforced with an 'orthostatic' curtain, so called because of its skirting of vertical limestone blocks from the Sarno valley. The choice of this tougher material even in the Etruscan period suggests that Pompeii was threatened both by the Greeks and by the Samnites present in the Campania region.

From the mid-5th century almost up to the end of the 4th century B.C. the town did not mint its own coinage and no monuments from the period have been found, suggesting that it was ruled by some other power. The history of this era has yet to be unravelled, but the most probable explanation is that Pompeii, together with other towns in the area, was part of a league headed by the Alfaterni from nearby Nuceria.

However, Hellenistic culture made great inroads under the Samnite rule as a result of the influence of the Greek colonies throughout Campania.

URBAN DEVELOPMENT

Between the end of the 4th and the beginning of the 3rd centuries B.C. the Greek influence began to take hold in Pompeii, especially in the 4th century when the town began to spread out north and east from the Forum.

The actual layout of the town was also modified with the introduction of a geometric arrangement. Buildings were laid out along a main north-south road, the Via Stabiana, running down to the sea and two east-west roads, the Via Nola and the Via dell'Abbondanza. This new road layout divided the

Chronological table:

7th century B.C.	The Oscans found the first settlement.
6th century B.C.	Etruscan influence and growth of the town.
524 B.C.	The Greeks defeat the Etruscans at Cumae.
423 B.C.	The Samnites conquer Capua, then Cumae, and later the whole Campania region.
343 - 290 B.C.	Rome is victorious over the Samnites and assumes control of the Campania region.
218 - 203 B.C.	Hannibal invades Italy.
2nd century B.C.	Pompeii becomes an ally of Rome.
80 B.C.	Pompeii joins the revolt of the Italic towns against Rome, is defeated and becomes a Roman colony.
27 B.C.	Octavius takes power and becomes Augustus Caesar, the first Roman emperor.
59 A.D.	Fight in the Amphitheatre between the inhabitants of Pompeii and those of Nuceria.
62 A.D.	Pompeii is seriously damaged by an earthquake (grade 6 on the Richter scale).
79 A.D.	Eruption of Vesuvius and destruction of the town.

town up into regular blocks 130 metres in length. New 'insulae' (rectangular plots of land with one or more buildings, surrounded by four roads) came into being in the part of the town later called 'Regio VI', and the areas in the eastern part were probably also built at the same time. The development of the town from the late 3rd and early 2nd centuries B.C. onwards was also influenced by the influx of large numbers of people from nearby Nuceria and Capua after the war against Rome.

The long Samnite wars between 343 and 290 B.C. ended in victory for Rome and the whole Campania region fell under Roman rule. Pompeii had not taken part in the war and accepted the Roman conditions under which it became a 'confederate' town, keeping its free status and preserving its institutions and language.

POMPEII IS RENOVATED

While Rome was the undisputed power in the Mediterranean, trade increased considerably, especially with the rich countries in the East.

In the early 2nd century Pompeii experienced a boom in prosperity thanks to its role as a sort of warehouse for agricultural produce coming from the inland areas of Nola and Nuceria. Financial well-being and the spread of Hellenistic culture led to much rebuilding in the town for both practical and ornamental purposes.

The Etruscan **Temple of Apollo** was demolished to be replaced by a Corinthian temple with colou-

The Stabian Baths.

The Basilica.

Imaginary reconstruction of the Forum colonnade.

red-stone floors and a two-storey colonnade was built along three sides of the **Forum**.

The main **temple of Jupiter** was then built and the Temple of Apollo was embellished with a covered portico joining it to the Forum. This new look turned the Forum into the centre of Pompeii's religious, political and administrative life.

The **Basilica** was built for the administration of justice and the running of business, the **Macellum** provided an area for the public market, and the **Comitium** served for political and administrative affairs. However, the continuous line of 'tabernae' (shops) were not moved from their original position along the Forum's eastern side.

The sacred area of the **triangular Forum**, which housed the ancient temple dedicated to Athena, was also refurbished. It was almost entirely rebuilt and the surrounding area was given a triangular Doric portico, hence the name 'the Triangular Forum'.

The natural gradient of the lava outcrop sloping down towards the Via Stabiana was the site chosen for the theatre district and the small theatre or 'Odeion' was later built there. Behind this were a **Gymnasium** and the **temple** consecrated to the Egyptian deity **Isis**, confirming the fact that Samnite Pompeii had close commercial links with the East. Thermal baths and spas, which were one of the major attributes of Greek cities, were also built during this period of modernisation. Among them were the **Stabian Baths** and the Republican Baths, but no traces of the latter have ever been found.

THE ROMAN COLONY OF POMPEII

Pompeii's history took another turn during the Social war when the town allied itself with other Italic settlements against Rome to fight for its freedom. The rebellion was put down by Silla and Pompeii lost its status as a free Italic town.

The Romans invaded the town and proclaimed it a colony in 80 B.C., calling it Cornelia Veneria Pompeianorum (after Lucius Cornelius Silla - Silla's nephew - and the Goddess Venus of whom Silla was a devout follower). The town then underwent a new period of development and transformation. First and foremost, many of the soldiers who had fought in Silla's army were awarded plots of land, some of which were situated within the town walls, while others were in the area called Pagus Augustus Felix Suburbanus just outside the town to the north.

The clearest sign of 'Romanisation' was the transformation of the Temple of Jupiter into the **Capitolium** dedicated to the Capitoline triad of Jupiter, Juno and Minerva. The **temple of Venus** was also built at this time on the spur of the hill overlooking the sea. The **Forum Baths** were built behind the Capitolium and the Stabian Baths were renovated and extended. The **Odeion** was built in the nearby theatre to provide a venue for musical and literary recitals, and an **Amphitheatre** was erected against the wall in the southern part of the town.

The town's transformation was also partially influenced by changes in demographic conditions and the state of absolute peace that now characterised

Imaginary reconstruction of the Amphitheatre.

The Augustan aureus.

the area. The first change was a more intensive use of land: for example houses were now built with more than one floor and balconies and windows were introduced to provide openings onto the roads around the 'insulae'. The town's residents started building houses with views, such as the **Imperial Villa**, which were called 'town villas' because of their terraced structure. These villas were built in the southern and western areas, against the now unnecessary town wall.

THE SYMBOLS OF THE EMPIRE

The religious and cultural renewal imposed by Augustus Caesar from 20 B.C. onwards also had a visible impact on Pompeii. The process of falling in line with the Empire's new political identity meant that the temples of Augustus' favourite deities were further embellished and that worship of these deities became synonymous with worshipping the Emperor.

The town's wealthier citizens were called upon to finance works to embellish the cult areas and to make them more functional in accordance with the practice in Rome at that time. A dummvir (a high-ranking administrative officer) raised funds for the Temple of Apollo during the festivities in honour of the god by arranging bull-fights, boxing matches and mime shows in the Forum, in addition to making a public contribution of over ten thousand sesterces.

The **Temple of Venus** was rebuilt in marble and extended while the cult of the Emperor was further consolidated by the building of the **Temple of Vespasian** in the Forum. The temple was built of marble and, according to an inscription, dedicated to the genius of Augustus.

The **Temple of the Public Lares** (tutelary gods of the town) was built in the Forum during the imperial period of the Julio-Claudian dynasty. The adjo-

The Temple of Vespasian.

ining **Building of Eumachia**, seat of the corporation of wool-workers, was dedicated to the Concordia and to the Pietas Augusta. At the northern end of the Forum, the pre-existing Hellenistic building was turned into the **Macellum** or covered market, and this was also dedicated to the cult of the Emperor.

Another market used for the sale of cereals, the **Forum Olitorium**, was built at the far end of the Forum. Works for the construction of a public lavatory alongside this market were begun but never completed.

The **Capitolium**, which had once been the Samnite Temple of Jupiter, was also modified, with equestrian statues added on either side of the stairs.

The Forum area was cleared of the statues of the 'honoured Pompeians', and foundations were laid for monumental equestrian statues and 3 quadrigae dedicated to the Emperors.

The Forum's tuff-stone floor was replaced with large limestone slabs from the Sarno valley, while only part of the old tuff-stone colonnade was replaced with a double order of travertine columns comprising Doric columns in the lower order and Ionic columns in the upper one.

Various **honorary arches** were built to close off

the Forum but they actually served a dual purpose, acting as physical boundaries and also providing 'privileged' podiums for imperial statues. The large arch, known as the **Arch of Nero**, on the eastern side of the Capitolium is one such example.

The temples of the imperial cult were also built outside the Forum area, for example the **Temple of Fortuna Augusta** on the corner of Via del Foro and Via della Fortuna.

Thanks to the generosity of the Holconius brothers, the **theatre** was renovated and extended with the addition of an upper section to increase the capacity by a few hundred places and to provide seats for the less well-off.

The **large Gymnasium** with a swimming pool in the centre was built near the Amphitheatre.

Imaginary reconstruction of one of the shops on Via di Mercurio.

The Honorary Arch of Nero in the Forum.

Page 7 Imaginary reconstruction of the Arch of Nero.

One of the most important public works carried out served to link Pompeii to the Roman aqueduct. This meant that for the first time in six hundred years the townspeople did not have to use the wells dug into the lava or rely on collected rainwater for their daily water requirements.

The new water system made it possible to build the **Suburban Baths** outside the Porta Marina gate and the **Sarno Baths** south of the ancient part of the town on the hillside. The pre-existing **Stabian Baths** and the **Forum Baths** were modernised and after the earthquake of 62 A.D. the larger **Central Baths** were built on the sites of houses which had been destroyed.

SENATVS
POPVLVSQE POMPEIANORVM
DRNLQVSPBCFGH LRPXVSE PRNL
LFORSTVM NRLIP ERS

OMPEI ANTIQVI
ARCVS NERONIS

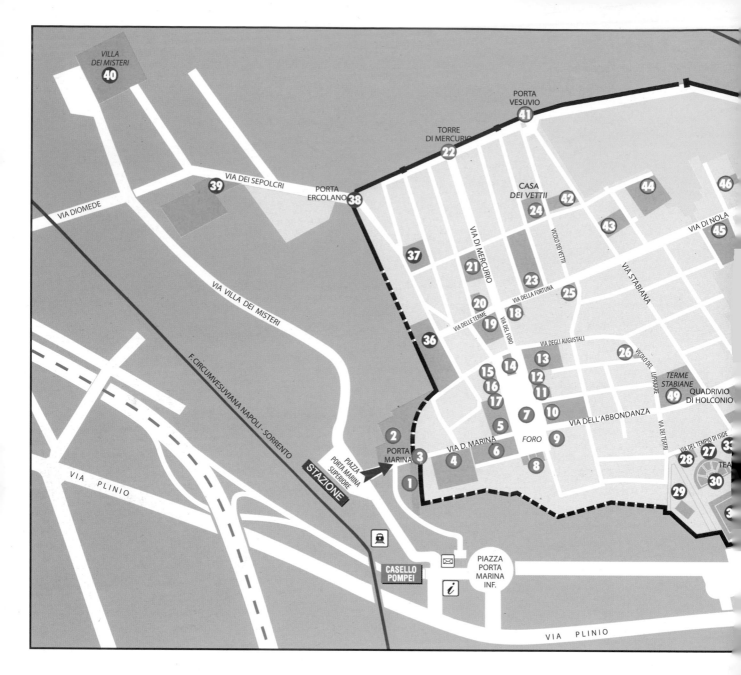

Map labels: VILLA DEI MISTERI 40, PORTA VESUVIO, TORRE DI MERCURIO 22, 41, VIA DEI SEPOLCRI, 39, VIA DIOMEDE, PORTA ERCOLANO 38, CASA DEI VETTII, 44, 46, 42, 24, 43, VIA DI NOLA, 45, VICOLO DEI VETTII, VIA DI MERCURIO, 37, VIA STABIANA, VIA VILLA DEI MISTERI, 21, 23, VIA DELLA FORTUNA, 25, 20, 18, VIA DELLE TERME, 19, VIA DEL FORO, 36, VIA DEGLI AUGUSTALI, 26, VICOLO DEL LUPANARE, TERME STABIANE, 13, 14, 12, 49, QUADRIVIO DI HOLCONIO, F. CIRCUMVESUVIANA NAPOLI - SORRENTO, 15, 16, 11, 17, 7, 10, VIA DELL'ABBONDANZA, VIA DEI TEATRI, 5, 2, 9, VIA DEL TEMPIO DI ISIDE, PORTA MARINA, 3, VIA D. MARINA, FORO, 28, 27, 4, 6, 8, 29, 30, PIAZZA PORTA MARINA SUPERIORE, STAZIONE, 1, VIA PLINIO, CASELLO POMPEI, PIAZZA PORTA MARINA INF., VIA PLINIO

Index of the Buildings

1 Imperial Villa
2 Suburban Baths
3 Porta Marina Gate
4 Temple of Venus
5 Temple of Apollo
6 Basilica
7 Forum
8 Municipal Buildings
9 Comitium
10 Building of Eumachia
11 Temple of Vespasian
12 Temple of the Public Lares
13 Macellum
14 Temple of Jupiter
15 Forum Public Toilets
16 Forum Grain Stores
17 Mensa Ponderaria
18 Temple of Fortuna Augusta
19 Forum Baths
20 House of the Tragic Poet
21 House of the Large Fountain
22 Tower of Mercury
23 House of the Faun
24 House of the Vettii
25 House of the Ancient Hunt
26 Lupanar (Brothel)
27 Temple of Isis
28 Samnite Gymnasium
29 Triangular Forum
30 Large Theatre
31 Gladiators' Barracks
32 Odeion
33 Temple of Jupiter Meilichios
34 House of the Ceii
35 House of Menander
36 House of Fabius Rufus
37 House of Sallust
38 Porta Ercolano Gate
39 Villa of Diomedes
40 Villa of Mysteries
41 Porta Vesuvio Gate
42 House of the Gilded Cupids
43 House of Caecilius Jucundus
44 House of the Silver Wedding
45 House of the Centenary
46 House of M. Lucretius Fronto
47 House of M. Obellius Firmus
48 Porta Di Nola Gate
49 Stabian Baths
50 House of the Lyre-Player
51 Laundry of Stephanus
52 Thermopolium
53 Asellina's Tavern'
54 House of the Ephebe
55 Bakery of Sotericus
56 Garum Workshop
57 House of Magical Rites
58 House of Octavius Quartius
59 House of Venus
60 House of Julia Felix
61 Porta Nocera Gate
62 Garden of the Fugitives
63 Amphitheatre
64 Large Palaestra

Legend:
2-hour visit
4 hour visit
Full-day visit

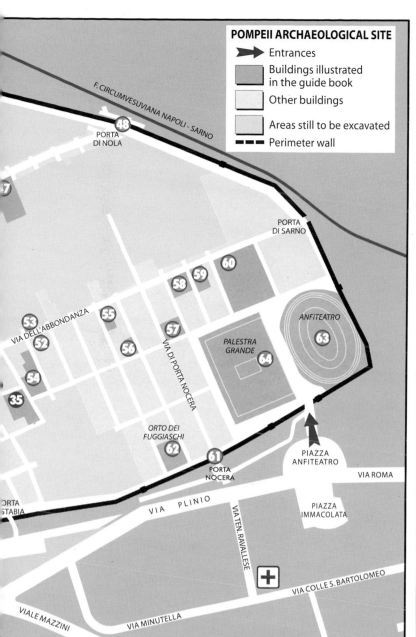

POMPEII ARCHAEOLOGICAL SITE

➤➤ Entrances

▓ Buildings illustrated in the guide book

▒ Other buildings

░ Areas still to be excavated

▪▪▪ Perimeter wall

THE DEATH OF POMPEII

THE PREMONITORY EARTHQUAKE

In 62 A.D., seventeen years before Pompeii was buried by the catastrophic eruption of Mount Vesuvius, a violent earthquake devastated the town. A large number of people must surely have died, and houses, public buildings and temples suffered considerable damage.

Thanks to its flourishing economy and to contributions of patrons with political ambitions, Pompeii quickly began to repair the damage that the areas of public interest had suffered.

The reconstruction work also included the houses, some of which were not only repaired, but extended and refurbished.

When the final catastrophe came, some of the reconstruction work was still in progress, as can be seen from the remains of building sites still open in various parts of the town.

However, a recently elaborated theory seems to shed some doubt on what were previously considered chronological certainties in the town's history. This theory suggests that Pompeii was hit by a second violent earthquake a few years before the eruption of Vesuvius, but long after the 62 A.D. earthquake. Recent excavations in some of the houses in Via dell'Abbondanza and Via Nocera have brought to light carpenters' tools and traces of 'cementum', which would seem to confirm that work was in progress to repair recent damage, whereas the restoration work had been completed following the earthquake of 62 A.D.

THE ERUPTION OF 79 A.D.

"A cloud formed..., the only way I can describe it is to say that its appearance and shape were similar to that of a cluster pine tree". This is the apocalyptic image of Vesuvius that met the eyes of the terrified inhabitants on the morning of Pompeii's final day, the 24th of August 79 A.D.. Up until then the volcano had been thought of merely as a luxuriantly green mountain.

We owe this description to Pliny the Younger, admiral of the Roman fleet stationed at Miseno and an expert naturalist who, in two letters to Tacitus, tells of the death of his uncle, Pliny the Elder. Pliny the Younger left Miseno with a few ships to help evacuate the inhabitants of the area and to witness the extraordinary volcanic phenomenon at first hand. He headed for Stabiae where his friend Pomponianus had a villa, and it was here that he lived through the emotion of the cataclysm.

"Continuous and prolonged tremors shook the house," he wrote in his first letter to Tacitus. "It was almost as if it were being pulled up from its foundations; one moment it seemed lower, the next higher. However, people were afraid of the shower of lapilli stones falling outside, however light and porous they might be; ... he chose to go outside ... he put some pillows on his head and secured them with sheets."

Another hypothesis is that at the time of the catastrophe, a number of houses had been abandoned for quite some time, not because of the building works but because the people had become mortally afraid to live in the town due to the series of minor earthquakes that had hit the area in the years leading up to 79 A.D..
The reconstruction of Pompeii was certainly not a 'transparent' operation, to use a modern term, and the emperor Vespasian had to send his prefect, Titus Suedius Clemens, to settle disputes regarding the illegal occupation of public land by private citizens.

Letter from Pliny the Younger to Tacitus.

Bas-relief on the Lararium in the house of the banker Caecilius Jucundus.

The body of Pliny the Elder was found on the beach at Stabiae. It is not certain if he died from inhaling the poisonous gases or was drowned in the tidal wave that probably hit the Gulf of Naples after the eruption.

That August morning the 'plug' of solidified lava that had formerly sealed the volcano's summit was ripped apart by the huge build up of pressure below.

The noise of the eruption was both deafening and terrifying.

This was followed by a prolonged shower of small lapilli (pumice stones) and then of volcanic ash which settled over a 70 kilometre radius to the south east.

Pompeii was buried under a two and a half metres thick layer of lapilli stones. The first layer was about one metre thick and was white (typical of the 79 A.D. eruption), while the second layer was grey.

Volcanic material fell for four days, during which time frequent tremors caused buildings to collapse and left little possibility of survival for the estimated 10,000-strong population.

However, most of the inhabitants of Pompeii were killed not by the collapsing buildings or the volcanic shower of stones and ash, but by the poisonous gases released from the pumice stones. We can see some of the tragic death scenes in the plaster casts made by archaeologists using Giuseppe Fiorelli's technique. To recreate the figures at the moment of their death the archaeologist poured liquid plaster into the hollows left in the ash when the bodies had decomposed. This technique can be used for any

Plaster cast of a victim of the eruption.

Villa dei Misteri Plaster cast of a door.

Stratigraphic cross-section of the eruption.

material that decomposes, particularly wood, and has allowed plaster casts to be made of doors, windows, stairs and other parts of the houses in Pompeii. A recent innovation in this technique has been used to obtain a cast of the body of a woman found in the ruins at Oplontis near Torre Annunziata.

The cast was made using glass fibre, which allowed the skeleton to be seen along with some of the jewels the woman was wearing as she attempted to escape.

THE DAY AFTER

A few days after the eruption an imperial commission of senators arrived in the Mount Vesuvius area to assess the damage and organise aid for the people. The land all the way from Naples to Stabiae was covered in a blanket of dark ash. There were no longer any houses, roads or trees. All forms of life had been wiped out.

The commission asked the Emperor Titus to help in repairing the damage to the town.

In 80 A.D. the Emperor came in person to the disaster areas but decided not to undertake any work in favour of the irredeemably buried towns of Pompeii and Herculaneum.

The inhabitants who had survived the disaster were the first to begin excavations at Pompeii in an attempt to recover statues of their Gods and sacred objects from the ruins of their homes.

The site of Pompeii remained barren and the inhabitants looked elsewhere for refuge, abandoning the now-inhospitable place for ever.

In 106 A.D., Titus wrote his 'Histories' and published the letters of an eye-witness to the tragedy, Pliny the Younger.

In one of his works the Emperor Marcus Aurelius (121-180 A.D.) referred to the fate of the towns as an example of the frailty and precarious nature of our earthly existence.

In the early 3rd century the historian Dion Cassius gave a new account of the catastrophe which had

In 88 A.D. the poet Martial visited the places destroyed by the eruption of Vesuvius and evoked the tragedy thus: "Everything lies buried under flames and sad ash. Not even the Gods could have wished such a scourge."

become news once again following another violent explosion of Vesuvius.

The emperor Alexander Severus (208-235 A.D.) began excavations to recover marble, columns and statues, but the works were soon interrupted. From then on Pompeii was completely forgotten. All that was left of the towns were vague directions on Roman maps, such as the Tabula Peutingeriana, which were reproduced up to the Middle Ages.

MOUNT VESUVIUS

The eruption of 79 A.D. radically changed the shape of the volcano. The steep volcanic cone collapsed leaving a crater with a perimeter of 11 kilometres. Today this is known as Mount Somma and is 1,132 metres high. Inside this, a new cone formed rising to 1,277 metres to give the modern-day appearance of the volcano.

Vesuvius erupted eleven times in the following 12 centuries, most violent occurred in 1139 of these eruptions.

The eruptions then became less frequent and in the 14th century there was a long period of inactivity. During this time the volcano was covered in lush vegetation.

In the late 16th century there were various tremors

During the Middle Ages Mount Vesuvius was considered "the mouth of hell".

which were almost a forewarning of the catastrophic eruption that was to take place on 16 December 1631. This eruption was almost equal in violence to that of 79 A.D. and caused the deaths of approximately 4,000 people.

Other violent eruptions followed, such as the one in 1707 when the Austrian garrison was stationed in Naples, and that of 1794 which destroyed Torre del Greco. There were other major eruptions in 1895 and 1899. Then came the eruptions of 1906 and 1944, the sad memories of which still live on in the minds of the people living around Mount Vesuvius.

1845 saw the setting up of the Mount Vesuvius Observatory near the crater at Herculaneum. It is a scientific station which keeps a constantly vigilant eye on the volcano's activity as Vesuvius certainly cannot be said to be completely dormant. This can be seen from the wisps of smoke inside the crater and from a moderate amount of seismic activity.

View of Vesuvius and the Gulf of Naples from Mount Faito.

The crater of Vesuvius.

THE DISCOVERY OF POMPEII

In the 16" century **Count Muzio Tuttavilla** commissioned reclamation works in the Sarno river valley with the aim of digging a canal. During the excavations, **the architect Fontana** found some buildings with decorated walls in the area known as 'Collina della Civita'. This find was documented and left at that, and the works on the canal continued. Excavations in Pompeii began again in 1748 under the reign of Charles of Bourbon while the excavations already under way at Herculaneum were heralding sensational discoveries. The digs at Pompeii were a monumental effort, with resources channelled into the greatest excavation work ever carried out. With a few brief interruptions, it has continued up to the present day. As Herculaneum was covered by a mud slide, excavation work made better progress in Pompeii because it was much harder to remove the hardened blanket of solidified mud than it was to dig out Pompeii from the layers of ash and lapilli stones. Interest in the research at Pompeii was given new vigour when many of the buildings around the Forum and some of the prestigious houses were found between 1806 and 1832.

In 1860 **Giuseppe Fiorelli** was appointed director of the archaeological site at Pompeii and he first introduced a methodology which combined discovery with the concept of conservation. This technique was applied to all the excavations in progress, which from then onwards were no longer single-mindedly inspired by the sole desire to find precious objects and important buildings.

For the first time the wish to bring one of history's greatest towns back to life led to rational and well-planned house-to-house excavations. A digging technique, whereby excavations began at roof level and moved down towards the floor layer by layer, was introduced to prevent buildings from collapsing outwards onto the previously excavated roads.

An important phase of research followed between

Excavation work in progress in the Temple of Isis.

1875 and 1893 under the direction of the **architect Michele Ruggiero**. Many insulae were uncovered as were numerous houses in the areas known as 'REGIO V', 'REGIO VIII' and 'REGIO IX' but, more importantly, restoration work began on over five hundred fresco paintings found on the walls of the houses.

The works went through a delicate phase under the direction of **Vittorio Spinazzola** and excavations carried out between 1910 and 1924 focused on the southern areas of the town. The aim of this was to unearth the whole stretch of the main road, Via dell'Abbondanza, bringing to light the facades of the buildings along the road and joining the Amphitheatre to the Forum. This caused problems in containing the facades of the buildings as they were now under pressure from the large quantities of ash inside them.

Furthermore, the fact that researchers continually found interesting items meant that they would at times begin to dig into the insulae out of sheer curiosity and then abandon them. Thus today we find several houses that have been only partially excavated. Then came the archaeologist **Amedeo Maiuri** who was responsible for the discovery of many items between 1924 and 1961 and, above all, the author of numerous studies and fundamental interpretations. It is thanks to him that many important chapters have been written in the great book of archaeology that we call Pompeii.

Giuseppe Spano, a figure from the academic world who worked as the director of the archaeological digs during Maiuri's superintendency, was the author of many works that have helped in understanding the history of the settlements around Mount Vesuvius.

The contemporary period has been characterised not only by new discoveries, but also by serious problems regarding the preservation of what was found in the past (regardless of the state of the national economy the Italian State has shown great reluctance to spend public money in this sector), and by the need to open up new chapters in the history of Pompeii as part of an interdisciplinary approach.

Aerial view of the Forum.

Itinerary 1

FROM THE PORTA MARINA GATE TO THE FORUM

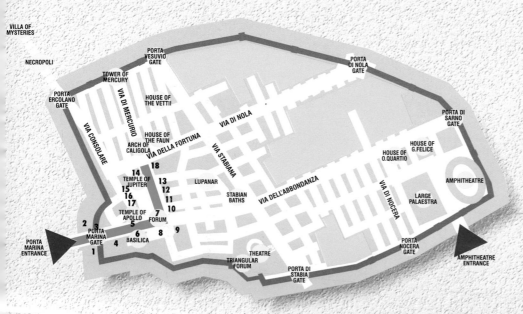

1	IMPERIAL VILLA
2	SUBURBAN BATHS
3	PORTA MARINA GATE
4	TEMPLE OF VENUS
5 **	TEMPLE OF APOLLO
6 *	BASILICA
7 **	FORUM
8	MUNICIPAL BUILDINGS
9	COMITIUM
10 *	BUILDING OF EUMACHIA
11 *	TEMPLE OF VESPASIAN
12	TEMPLE OF THE PUBLIC LARES
13	MACELLUM
14 *	TEMPLE OF JUPITER
15	FORUM PUBLIC TOILETS
16	FORUM GRAIN STORES
17	MENSA PONDERARIA
18	TEMPLE OF FORTUNA AUGUSTA

* *worth seeing*
** *not to be missed*

In the upper part of the living-room front wall: small painting with panel doors decorated in the third style.

The flight of Daedalus and the fall of Icarus. Detail of the nymph.

① THE IMPERIAL VILLA

This is one of the patrician houses which were built in the shelter of the town walls during the first imperial age. The various rooms of the residence are laid out in terraces descending the natural slope of the hill on which the town of Pompeii was founded and thus enjoy a fine view over the Gulf of Naples. The villa was destroyed by the earthquake of 62 A.D. and was never rebuilt although a number of significant features are still visible today: these include the 80-metre-long colonnade with its 43 columns. Although these are no longer intact, they were originally decorated with white stucco to create a fluted effect and stood out sharply against the rear wall with its black square panels (which were unfortunately removed during the 18th century). The colonnade led westwards into the villa's residential quarters, which included a large living room and triclinium (measuring 6 metres by 8.80 metres), an alcove with windows looking out to sea, and several other smaller rooms. The vestibulum and the vault of the living room are embellished with rectangular and octagonal coffered decorations with bas-relief figures and fourth style ornamentation, whilst third style decoration was used for the three walls which are embellished with panel motifs and a frieze of cherubs and vine shoots in the lower section beneath the typical vermillion painted wall and small Greek-style frescoes of figure scenes framed inside niches. The rear wall depicts the legend of Theseus slaying the Minotaur: the left-hand wall portrays Theseus abandoning Ariadne while on the right-hand wall we can see the flight of Daedalus and the fall of Icarus. A series of small paintings with panel doors complete the decoration at the top.

Theseus slaying the Minotaur, with the city of Athens and a statue of the goddess Athena in the background.

② THE SUBURBAN BATHS

These stood just outside the town walls, which can be seen to the left of the road leading to the Porta Marina gate, and possibly near a canal port, which is suggested by the mooring rings set in stone blocks. The baths are laid out on three levels and are now visible in all their former glory thanks to recent restoration work. The baths complex was not actually very big and was probably used by people coming from outside the town. The entrance hall stood on a terrace with a colonnade which could be reached by a flight of stairs.

All the rooms in the complex had windows looking out over the Gulf of Naples and were laid out according to the classic criteria for bathing chambers which here culminate in a large hot-water pool. Thus we find the entrance hall followed by the changing room (apodyterium), two rooms for taking cold baths (frigidarium) a heated chamber (tepidarium) which enabled bathers to get acclimatized to the change in temperature before entering the hot-water bath (calidarium).

The walls of the changing room were decorated with eight fresco paintings of a highly erotic nature. This initially led archaeologists to the conclusion that this area must have been a brothel annexed to the baths, but this apparently obvious interpretation has been rejected in favour of another explanation.

In this case, the erotic frescoes were probably a humourous method of reminding customers where they had left their clothes by assigning a number and an amusing painting to each of the various chambers.

Imaginary reconstruction of the Temple of Venus.

③ THE PORTA MARINA GATE

Once the gateway into the town from the harbour, it is now the main entrance into the archaeological site. The steep slope must have made this a somewhat difficult climb, but it was the only way of linking the harbour to the Forum. The gate itself is incorporated into a tower with two arched passageways: one was served by stairs for pedestrians while the other was both wider and higher and was used by carts and wagons. The tunnel itself has a single barrel vault which opens out onto Via Marina and runs alongside the Temple of Venus.

④ THE TEMPLE OF VENUS

This was the temple of the goddess to whom Silla dedicated the colony in calling it Cornelia Veneria Pompeianorum. The building, made entirely of marble, was situated in the part of the town with the best view out to sea and was clearly visible to ships. Little of the temple now remains as a result of the damage it suffered in the earthquake of 62 A.D. and also because it was stripped of its marble after the eruption of 79 A.D.. The shrine was closed off by a high wall and could be reached by the entrance in the north eastern corner on Via Marina. The temple stood on a podium measuring approximately 30 metres by 15 metres and was surrounded by a portico with two rows of columns on the longer sides and one row on the northern wall. The eastern side of the temple was embellished by two pedestals with statues and provided access to the houses at the foot of the slope where the priests of Venus probably lived.

The Porta Marina. The gate linked the town to the harbour on the coast.

The Suburban Baths.

Detail of the statue of Apollo.

Bust of Diana

The 'cella' or inner sanctuary of the Temple. The particularly beautiful floor was made with coloured marble. To the left the omphalos, an oval shaped block representing the 'umbilicus of the world', the attribute of the Apollo of Delphi.

⑤ THE TEMPLE OF APOLLO ✳✳

In a sacred site on the corner of Via Marina and the Forum we find the temple dedicated to the god Apollo. This cult was of Greek origin and spread as a source of worship among the Italic peoples through the Greek colonies in this part of Italy.

The cult had probably been present in Pompeii ever since the town was founded in the 6ᵗʰ century B.C., as is suggested by the fragments of Attic and Corinthian pottery and the remains of Etruscan bowls found during archaeological excavations. Interest in the cult of Apollo began to dwindle in Pompeii in the 5ᵗʰ century B.C. but the ancient temple survived for a further 3 centuries before being replaced by a new structure erected on a podium built inside a portico with 48 columns of tuff stone quarried in the nearby town of Nuceria (Nocera). The temple was surrounded by Corinthian columns with a travertine stone altar at the foot of the long flight of stairs and a sun dial slightly to one side. During the reign of the Emperor Nero after the earthquake of 62 A.D. the columns and trabeation were embellished with stucco work, only a few remains of which are now visible.

The doors leading from the temple directly into the Forum were closed when the townspeople's cult interest passed to the Temple of Jupiter, which was later transformed into the Capitolium, and niches were built in their place, as can still be seen. Statues of divinities stood around the portico but those on view today are copies. To the right of the long side of the portico we find the bronze statue of Apollo with a bow and arrow opposite a bust of Diana. Alongside the columns marking the entrance to the temple stood two statues: Venus and a small altar on one side and a Hermaphrodite on the other.

Portico of the Temple of Apollo.

Statue of Apollo

View of the Temple of Apollo.

Imaginary Reconstruction of the Temple of Apollo.

TEMPLVM·APOLLINIS·

Detail of the double order of columns in the Tribunal.

⑥ THE BASILICA ✳

Contrary to tradition, the main entrance into the Basilica was on the short side of the building at the intersection of Via Marina and the Forum, although there are two small doors on the longer sides. This majestic building from the 2nd century B.C. housed the town's law courts and, according to an engraving found during archaeological digs, was called the 'bassilica'.

However it is quite likely that this was also a place where businessmen would make deals, a sort of 'stock market' in the centre of a town in which commercial trading played a crucial role in the local economy. The Basilica was always a hive of activity with large numbers of people bustling about their daily business here as if the place were a sort of covered Forum. Evidence of this can be seen in the hundreds of examples of graffiti, including some particularly vulgar expressions scratched onto the walls.

The spacious central area, bounded on all four sides by 28 wide brick columns 11 metres in height, was covered by a tile roof. The side walls were decorated with first style stucco work and Ionic semi-columns. A gallery stood on top of this with large openings in its outer walls to let daylight into the Basilica.

On the side opposite the entrance and projecting slightly from the building's rectangular perimeter, there is a small dais that stands about 2 metres higher than the surrounding area and seems to have been an altar. In front of this were six Corinthian columns, two of which were joined to sections of wall creating two side chambers. This raised area was probably the tribunal which, as it was not linked to the main area in any way, must have been a sacred aedicula containing statues of gods.

The judicial functions on the other hand, were probably carried out in the chambers set on either side from which staircases also led into the crypt below the podium. In actual fact the most likely interpretation is that this was where the magistrate would sit during trials and the lack of a permanent staircase can be explained by the need to guarantee the judge's isolation and safety from the frequently violent reactions of the citizens standing trial. Hence a wooden staircase was probably provided.

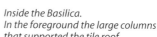

Inside the Basilica.
In the foreground the large columns that supported the tile roof.

Aerial view.

The large covered areas of the Basilica were a favourite meeting-place for the townspeople.

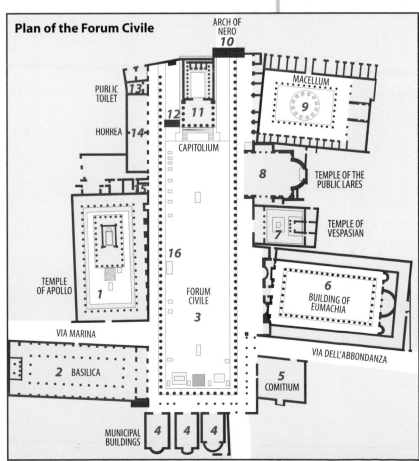

Plan of the Forum Civile

ARCH OF NERO
10

PUBLIC TOILET

13

HORREA
14

12

11

CAPITOLIUM

MACELLUM
9

8

TEMPLE OF THE PUBLIC LARES

TEMPLE OF APOLLO
1

16

7

TEMPLE OF VESPASIAN

6
BUILDING OF EUMACHIA

FORUM CIVILE
3

VIA MARINA

VIA DELL'ABBONDANZA

2 BASILICA

5
COMITIUM

MUNICIPAL BUILDINGS

4 **4** **4**

The Arch of Nero.

Previous page: Forum.

⑦ THE FORUM ✱✱

From the Porta Marina gate, Via Marina climbs up steeply towards the Forum which was the main square in Pompeii and was reserved exclusively for pedestrians as all vehicles were forbidden entry. This was the very heart of Pompeii's daily life and housed the most important municipal, religious and commercial buildings in the town, in addition to being the intersection of the main streets. Around the Forum we find the town's most important temples, the public offices where the administrative authorities governed the town, as well as legal offices and a few markets.

There were no private houses at all.
Before illustrating each of these it is worth describing the actual space the Forum occupies.
The forum runs north-south for 142 metres and is 38 metres wide. As it had always been the seat of political and religious power, its buildings were frequently modified to reflect new construction techniques or fashions, cultural and political influences and also changes in cult worship.
The architecture in the Forum was characterized by a colonnade on three sides while the fourth side provided an uninterrupted view of the Temple of Jupiter. It was paved with travertine stone slabs, only

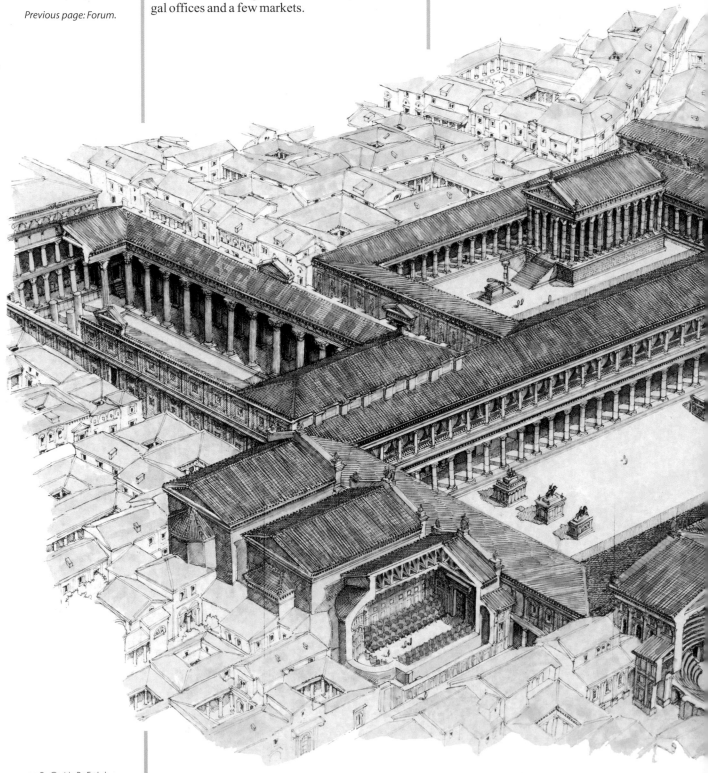

a few traces of which now remain. Originally the colonnade consisted of a double order of Nuceria tuff-stone columns with Doric columns in the lower order and Ionic columns in the upper one.

A few remains of these can be seen in the southern part of the Forum, while the western part preserves traces of the stairs leading up to the open gallery. The travertine stone colonnade was started in the Julio-Claudian age but was never completed.

The bases of numerous statues are visible in the Forum. On these stood equestrian statues of emperors and influential citizens of the town and include the Suggestum, which was used for speaking to the townspeople. However, not a single statue was ever found. After the earthquake of 62 A.D. the Forum became a huge building site to repair the damage it had suffered and all the statues were transferred elsewhere.

Moreover, it is thought that the Forum, like other parts of the town, was stripped of its marble and even its floor immediately after the eruption of 79 A.D. On either side of the Temple of Jupiter the Forum was closed by two arches topped with equestrian statues. The arch on the right-hand side is thought to be dedicated to Nero.

The colonnade around the Forum.

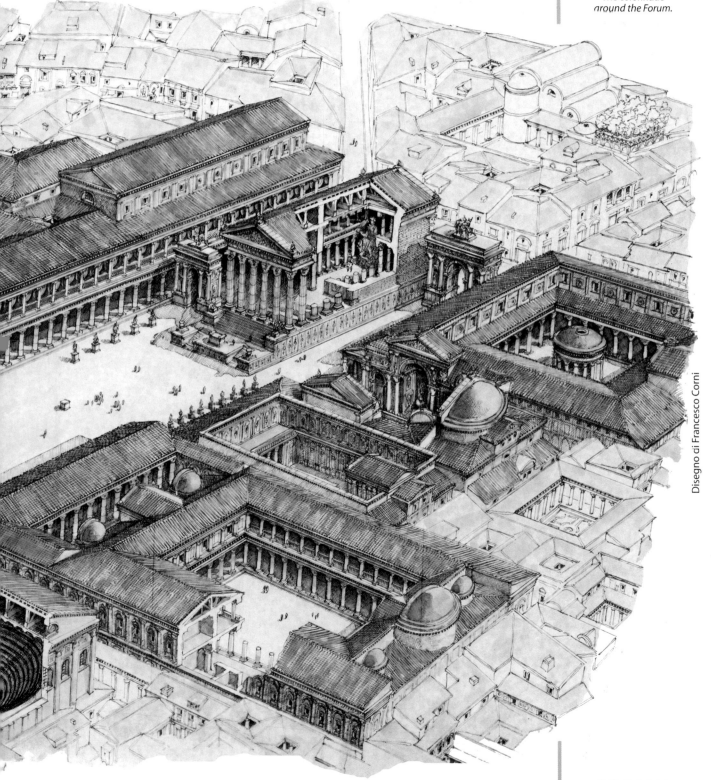

Disegno di Francesco Corni

8 THE MUNICIPAL BUILDINGS

Three almost identical buildings situated on the southern side of the Forum were the seat of the town's municipal offices. The most important of these were the Office of the Duumviri, the highest authority in the town, the Office of the Aediles, who were responsible for public works and maintenance of town buildings, the Council of Decurions, who acted as town councillors, and the municipal archives.

While archaeologists are certain of the general function of the complex, opinion is divided on the actual use of the individual buildings. The first on the right, in the corner where the Basilica stands, was probably the Curia, seat of the Ordo Decurionum or town council. This building still preserves its marble floor and has an apse on the far wall, while the side walls have three rectangular niches where honorary statues of emperors or eminent citizens of Pompeii once stood. The central building was probably the Office of the Duumviri, although some scholars think it might have been the seat of the Council of Decurions. An unusual feature can be seen in the small columns marking out the presence of a podium on which stood wooden cabinets housing administrative files and archives. Finally, the third building has been attributed as the Office of the Aediles.

*Two views
of the Municipal Buildings.*

9 THE COMITIUM

In the corner where Via dell'Abbondanza enters the Forum we find a building that acted as a sort of polling station for municipal elections. The original building could be reached via five entrances in the northern wall and five in the eastern one so that voters could enter from the Forum and go straight out into Via dell'Abbondanza. However, after the earthquake of 62 A.D. only three entrances were used: one in the north wall and two leading to the Forum. On the southern side of the building we find a podium where the magistrates sat when presiding over the electoral proceedings, while the other two walls contained niches housing honorary statues.

Town Administration

"PLEASE VOTE FOR HIM"

"O V F", this was the customary abbreviation used at the end of a text of electoral propaganda painted on the walls of the town in an appeal to the electorate ("oro vos faciatis" - "please vote for him") so that this or that candidate would be elected to one of the four posts in the town's administration.

Hustings would be held in the town every March so that the electorate could decide which candidate to vote for in the April elections of the two 'duumviri iure dicundo' and the two 'aediles', who would then take up office on the first of July. The Duumviri were the town's highest-ranking magistrates and were responsible for the political running of the town and the administration of justice. It was their job to ensure the implementation of the resolutions passed by what we can call the 'town council' (ordo decurionum) which was made up of 100 members, elected every five years according to their status in terms of wealth and acknowledged honours.

Lesser but nevertheless important tasks were carried out by the aediles who were responsible for organising the works and activities needed for the daily running of the town. These included organising the town market, town planning and roads, maintenance of public and religious buildings, the baths and the organisation of public games.

The *Comitium*, in the corner between the **Forum** and **Via dell'Abbondanza**, served as a polling station where the electorate (men only) would go during elections with their 'tesserula', a sort of polling card attesting to the voter's identity. Voters were required to write down the name of the chosen candidate on a waxed tablet which was then placed in the ballot box. The candidates that had attained the relative majority of votes in the most electoral constituencies would be elected. For instance, a candidate would not be elec-

Electoral slogans. Almost everyone allowed the walls of their house or the front wall of their shop to be whitewashed and then used for the electoral propaganda of their chosen candidate.

Electoral slogans on the walls of Via dell'Abbondanza. The electoral propaganda was written on the walls by the 'scriptores' in response to a request not by the candidates themselves but by the people (ordinary citizens, corporations or local religious organisations) who intended to support the candidature of someone whom they considered worthy of holding public office.

ted if he got the maximum votes in just a few constituencies and no votes at all in the others. In the event of a tied vote, the winner would be chosen on the basis of whether he was married and how many children he had. The whole town took a keen interest in the election campaign, as can be seen from the many inscriptions found on the walls. Every category of workers, traders and businessmen had a steadfast commitment to taking part as well as a strong sense of civic responsibility to ensure that the worthiest candidates were elected. There must have been an almost full turn-out at every election, judging from the exhortations made on the electorate district by district, house by house and shop by shop.

"Be careful, be ready and get others to vote" is the heartfelt appeal in one inscription; elsewhere, supporters of some candidate appeal to other voters and indicate the name of their candidate for whom they hope to gain support.

Although women did not have the right to vote, they nevertheless played a crucial role given that they had a number of influential contacts through their work or social acquaintances.

The town's life and activity was run from three **Municipal Buildings** found in the southern part of the Forum, while the administration of justice was carried out by the Duumviri in the **Basilica**.

The wool-makers dedicated a statue to the priestess, whose family manufactured tiles and amphorae and also made wine. The statue is on display at the National Archaeological Museum in Naples.

Detail of the sculpted marble portal.

⑩ THE BUILDING OF EUMACHIA *

Continuing along the eastern side of the Forum, just after the junction with Via dell'Abbondanza, we find a majestic and elegant building with a marble frieze above the portal.

Two inscriptions - one on the marble colonnade in the Forum and another by the rear entrance in Via dell'Abbondanza - attribute this building to Eumachia, a priestess of Venus and owner of a flourishing business operating in the wool industry, which she had inherited from her husband.

Indeed, this is thought to be the seat of the Corporation of wool and cloth manufacturers, although another interpretation claims that the building was dedicated by the priestess to the Gens Iulia and was used for cult worship of the Emperor Augustus through the statues of his ancestors.

It may well be that the building served both commemorative and commercial functions.

The building itself dates from the Tiberian age and looks onto the Forum from a facade with two apses and four rectangular niches which, according to the fragments of inscriptions found here, housed the statues of the imperial family's ancestors: Aeneas, Romulus, Julius Caesar, the Emperor Augustus, as in the Augustan Forum in Rome.

Just inside the entrance, on the right we find a small room that was used as a urinal. Its location at the very centre of the Forum can be explained by the need to procure urine, which was used to bleach material in the manufacturing process.

A large courtyard inside the building was surrounded by a two-storey colonnade with an apse that housed a statue of the Concordia Augusta on a podium. On the other side of the colonnade wall with its large windows stood the three-sided cryptoporticus. Here, behind the apse, the statue of Eumachia was found in a niche adjacent to a small corridor leading to Via dell'Abbondanza, right in front of the fountain that gives its name to the street (the Street of Plenty).

Damaged during the earthquake of 62 A.D., the building had been only partially restored by the time of the eruption.

The Building of Eumachia.
The entrance from the Forum.

The room used for collecting urine.

Colonnade in front of the Building of Eumachia.

The Building of Eumachia is thought to have been the seat of the Corporation of wool and cloth manufacturers. The products of Pompeii's businesses were traded in the shelter provided by the colonnade, while the materials were stored in the cryptoporticus behind.

⑪ THE TEMPLE OF VESPASIAN *

This temple was built after the earthquake of 62 A.D. as a place of worship for the cult of the Emperor and has a facade projecting slightly further out than the building of Eumachia. A central door leads into a space in front of the inner sanctuary which is bounded on the front side by four columns. Inside these, a staircase on either side led up to a podium on which stood the cella containing the cult statue. Behind the sacellum were three rooms used for the officiators both of this temple and of the adjacent Temple of the Lares which could be reached via a communicating doorway. A marble altar with bas-relief sculptures can be seen in the centre of the sanctuary.

Temple of Vespasian.

Temple of Vespasian. Imaginary reconstruction.

Altar of the Temple of Vespasian. The decoration on the front depicts a sacrificial scene with a bull being led towards the high-priest, portrayed with a veil on his head and pouring out libations on a tripod. The scene is set against a temple in the background.
The side of the altar facing the cella portrays a crown of oak leaves identical to the one above the entrance to the House of the Emperor Augustus on the Palatine in Rome, and two bay trees.
The other two sides portray the sacred instruments.

12 THE TEMPLE OF THE PUBLIC LARES

This temple was built after the earthquake of 62 A.D. and was dedicated to Pompeii's tutelary gods as an act of expiation for the calamity the town had suffered. Although it had not been completed at the moment of the eruption, what remains suggests that its architecture was quite unusual. It was completely open on the side looking onto the Forum and could be reached through a portico adjoining the colonnade on the Forum, the bases of which are still visible. The temple had no roof and was floored with coloured marble arranged in a geometrical design. In the centre stood an altar, of which few remains can now be seen. In the rear wall a niche probably housed three statues of the town's gods. On either side of the entrance were two alcoves with inset niches where the statues of other Lares undoubtedly stood.

13 THE MACELLUM

In the north-eastern corner of the Forum stood the covered market where the townspeople could buy the food they needed. Built during the Augustan age, its main entrances in the Forum and Via degli Augustali were lined with shops. It originally had a secondary entrance on Vico del Balcone Pensile which was later closed off when the Temple of the Public Lares was built.
The entrance under the colonnade in the Forum was divided into two gateways by a votive aedicula and led into the open space which was originally surrounded by a portico. A number of shops opened out onto the right-hand side of the Macellum while the rear wall was divided into three areas. The central room acted as a 'sacellum' or shrine dedicated to the imperial household. It comprises four niches on the side walls (in which two unidentified statues were found) and a podium on the far wall. The left-hand chamber was used for sacrificial banquets while the room on the right with its long stone counter and drainage system was the fish market.

The Forum colonnade, behind which stood the shops looking onto the Macellum.

The Macellum. Twelve bases, in the centre, were used to support a roof under which a fountain was provided for cleaning the fish.

The colossal torso of the statue of Jupiter.

⑭ THE TEMPLE OF JUPITER *

The name of the temple derives from its original function in the Samnite period. Following the town's colonisation, the temple became a Capitolium, a temple dedicated to the capitoline triad of Jupiter, Juno and Minerva, in accordance with the religious tradition of Rome which required the centre of every town to have a temple dedicated to the most important gods on Mount Olympus.

With its dominant position in the Forum and lofty Mount Vesuvius looming ominously behind it, the Temple of Jupiter is an emblematic image of the destruction of Pompeii.

The Temple stands on an Italic podium measuring about 17 metres along the front by 37 metres down the sides and has rows of steps running along the whole facade looking onto the Forum. At the top of the steps, six columns - originally about 12 metres in height - led into an open space (the pronaos) which in turn led into the 'cella' or inner sanctuary. The cella was divided into three areas housing the statues of the capitoline triad.

The temple had two narrow flights of stairs, one on either side of a large central dais where the altar stood, and two monumental balustrades with equestrian statues. A bas relief portraying the temple during the earthquake was found in the lararium in the house of Caecilius Jucundus and gives us a glimpse of what the building was really like.

Under the podium was a series of small chambers where the temple's sacred furnishings, votive offerings and perhaps also the Treasury were stored.

The majestic architecture of the Temple of Jupiter which stands out against the impressive outline of Mount Vesuvius.

15 PUBLIC TOILETS

Just beyond an area in which archaeological material is stored, we can see a room that led into the public toilets, an indispensable facility in a particularly busy town square. Built in the town's final years, the lavatory is provided with a drain running around three of the walls above which wooden or stone seats were fitted. As was customary for the time, the toilets were set one next to another, not in individual cubicles.

16 GRAIN STORES

This building is currently closed by a gate and is used for storing archaeological findings. Originally, it was a market where the people of Pompeii could buy cereals, herbs and dried pulses. It opened out onto the Forum and had evidently not been completed at the time of the eruption as the walls show no sign of having ever been plastered.

The Forum grain stores.

17 THE MENSA PONDERARIA

This was where the standard weights and measures were stored. They were used to make sure that shopkeepers and traders were effectively selling their customers the correct weight or amount of produce.

Nine round holes in a limestone block situated in a niche on the outer wall of the Temple of Apollo were used as standard measures. Here, under the supervision of the town magistrates, produce was weighed by placing it in the round cavities and then removed via the holes made below the counter. This public service had already been introduced in the Samnite period, but after 20 B.C. the measures including three additional ones on a new counter - were adapted to the new parameters of the Roman system of weights and measures, as is explained on an inscription that the Duumviri had engraved on the stone block.

Stone measures.

*Mensa ponderaria.
The cavities dug out
of the counter correspond
to different weights.*

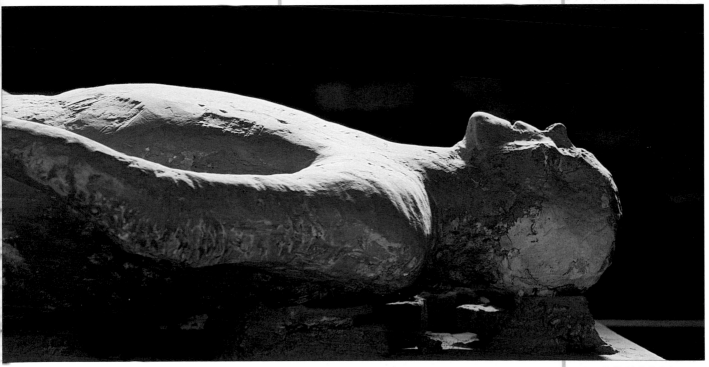

Reconstruction.

18 THE TEMPLE OF FORTUNA AUGUSTA

Leaving the Forum now and heading along Via del Foro to the corner of Via della Fortuna, we find the Temple of Fortuna Augusta built at the expense of Marcus Tullius, a relative of the famous orator Cicero. This benefactor, an eminent citizen of Pompeii and twice Duumvir in the Augustan age, even went so far as to create the position of ministers of the cult. The temple thus acquired a political connotation, which was spread through the diffusion of the imperial cult. Hence whenever a new emperor succeeded to the throne, the ministers immediately had a statue built and placed in the temple along with a stone slab to commemorate the event. This fairly small building, which was destroyed during the earthquake of 62 A.D. and was never fully rebuilt, had the same architectural layout as the Temple of Jupiter in the Forum. The cella was situated on a high podium and could be reached via a staircase containing a platform on which the altar stood. A niche on the rear wall of the cella housed the statue of Fortuna Augusta while honorary statues were placed in the four side niches.

Temple of the Fortuna Augusta.

Decoration with cupids in the House of the Vettii

Itinerary 2

FROM THE FORUM TO THE HOUSE OF THE VETTII

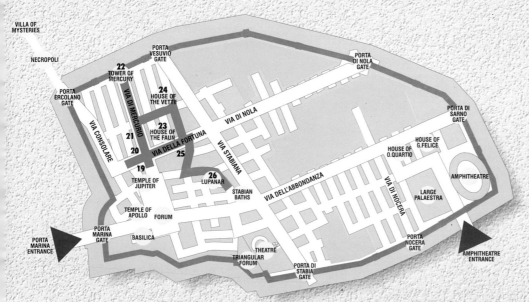

* worth seeing
** not to be missed

Marble labrum in the calidarium.

⑲ THE FORUM BATHS ✱✱

These baths were situated in Via delle Terme at the very centre of Pompeii in the building opposite the Temple of Fortuna Augusta. They were built in the first year of the founding of the colony with public funds and were always assiduously frequented by the town authorities. The damage suffered during the earthquake was immediately repaired, and they were in fact the only baths in use at the moment of the eruption in 79 A.D.. Although by no means a large establishment, the Forum baths were nevertheless equipped with all the bathing facilities that Roman citizens could desire.

The baths were subdivided into men's and women's sections, each with their own independent entrance. There were three doors leading to the men's baths on the streets around the building, but we cannot be sure which were entrances and which were exits.

The narrow corridor opening onto Via delle Terme led straight into the changing room and the entrances on Via del Foro and Vicolo delle Terme passed through a porticoed courtyard before reaching the changing room. The changing room (apodyterium) was provided with wooden wardrobes in which customers could leave their clothes and stone benches along the walls. It had a barrel vault roof with a skylight in one of the lunettes, and both the walls and the vaults were embellished with stucco decorations on a yellow background, of which only a few traces now remain.

The first chamber was the frigidarium where customers could take a cold bath. It is a square shaped room lit by an opening in the vault, with apsidal niches in the corners and a round bath with steps in the centre of the room. The changing room had another door leading into the tepidarium where customers could take a warm bath with water heated by a bronze brazier. This bathing chamber had a barrel vault ceiling while its walls were elegantly embellished with stucco work placed on either side of giants holding up a shelf.

Lastly came the calidarium with its hot water bath and, on the far wall, a marble labrum, a bath with cold water for guests who needed to cool off. The temperature in the room was maintained by the circulation of warm air (heated in an adjacent room which also housed the boilers for the hot water) in a cavity between the walls and a lining of breast-shaped tiles (tegulae mammatae). The women's baths were laid out in a similar way on the other side of the boiler room, which was used by both sections and could be reached from the entrance on Via delle Terme.

LAYOUT OF THE FORUM BATHS

1 Entrances/Exits
2 Apodyterium
3 Frigidarium
4 Tepidarium
5 Calidarium
6 Gymnasium
7 Women's section

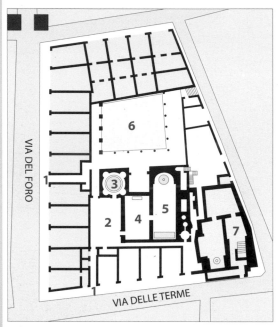

VIA DEL FORO

VIA DELLE TERME

Above: The frigidarium in the men's section. Below: the calidarium.

*The House of the Tragic Poet.
Reconstruction.*

⑳ THE HOUSE OF THE TRAGIC POET *

A mosaic depicting a growling dog and the well-known words of warning 'cave canem' (beware of the dog) is the decoration found near the entrance of this medium-sized, imperial style house opposite the Forum baths. The house has a Tuscan atrium and a peristyle with a lararium situated on the rear wall. The atrium leads into the cubicula (bedrooms) and the tablinum. The house derives its name from a fine mosaic with a theatrical scene which was found in this tablinum along with paintings representing episodes from the Iliad.

These finds are now exhibited at the National Archaeological Museum in Naples.

To the right of the peristyle we find the triclinium whose frescoes and figured panels are still intact. The panel on the rear wall depicts Ariadne abandoned by Theseus while the panel on the left-hand wall portrays a nest full of cupids.

21 THE HOUSE OF THE LARGE FOUNTAIN

The garden of this house is embellished with a large fountain decorated with coloured mosaics and compositions made of glass paste tiles.

Rows of shells running all round the nymphaeum form a highly original decoration which is completed by two large theatrical masks embedded in the bases of two columns.

The water for the fountain flowed through a hole in the middle of the apse and fell over a flight of marble steps, creating an impressive effect, before being collected in a small pool decorated with a bronze statue of a cupid carrying a dolphin on his back. The statue on display here is a copy.

The garden of the adjoining house, called **the House of the Small Fountain**, has large landscape paintings and a smaller fountain with decorations very similar to the ones in the previous house. Here the water flows out from a marble mask of Silenus.

The House of the Large Fountain. The ornate fountain.

The House of the Small Fountain.

22 THE TOWER OF MERCURY

From the top of this tower we can see the ruins of Pompeii from their highest point. This is one of the towers that were built into the town walls after the 3rd century as a vantage point from which to observe the whole town. In addition to the ground floor, it has two upper floors and a large embattled terrace from which patrols would set out for their rounds along the walls. The imprints left by the round stones hurled at the town by the catapults of Silla's army (90 B.C.) are still visible on the wall between the Porta Ercolano and the Porta Vesuvio gates. Two additional towers were later added to this section of the town walls.

A panel with dice players. This painting was found in one of the rooms of the inn (according to some a gambling den) just opposite the fountain of Mercury.

A view of Via di Mercurio with the Tower in the background.

23 THE HOUSE OF THE FAUN **

Covering a total surface area of about three thousand square metres, this building occupies a whole insula (block) and is certainly one of the largest and most sumptuous houses in Pompeii. Its entrance lies in Via della Fortuna. The residence is of Samnite origin and was built in the early 2nd century B.C. in place of an older construction. It derives its name from the small bronze statue of a dancing faun (a copy of which is exhibited here) which decorates the impluvium of the Tuscan atrium. Nothing is known about its owners.

From an architectural viewpoint this house is unique not only for its remarkable size, but also because it has two atria, two peristyles, four triclinia and a small bathing complex. Each of the two distinct parts of the house was arranged around an atrium of its own.

The first part, which has a Tuscan atrium, is identified by the greeting "Have" which appears both in a mosaic on the pavement and on the 1st style decorations of the entrance hall. This was certainly the residential section of the house, while the other, laid out around a tetrastyle atrium, was where the servants lived and worked.

Opposite the entrance to the residential section is a tablinum whose floor is decorated with a cube design in perspective. The skeleton of a woman carrying jewels and coins was found in this room and is assumed to have been the wealthy owner of the house. The house has two winter triclinia, one on either side of the tablinum, and a first peristyle with 27 stuccoed columns just behind the tablinum itself. Two co-lumns mark the entrance to the exedra in which the magnificent mosaic depicting a scene from the battle of Issus between Alexander the Great and King Darius of Persia was found.

A corridor from one of the two summer triclinia which extend all round the exedra leads to a larger peristyle with 48 Doric columns. This has a lararium on the left and the door to the gardener's lodgings on the right. A secondary entrance to the house from Vicolo di Mercurio also leads into this peristyle. In the servants' quarters, which can be reached through separate doors from two shops, we can see a number of cubicula where the staff slept. The kitchen, the lavatory and the small private baths of the house opened onto a narrow passageway leading to the peristyle. The baths are composed of a tepidarium and a calidarium which used the heat generated by the hearth in the adjoining kitchen and both had slightly raised floors.

A detail from the famous mosaic of the battle of Issus between Alexander the Great and King Darius of Persia. It is probably the copy of a Hellenistic painting and is made from over one and a half million tiles. It is now exhibited at the National Archaeological Museum in Naples.

A copy of the bronze statue of the dancing faun.

A view of the atrium with its impluvium.

The first internal garden of the house and, in the background, the entrance to the second peristyle.
An imaginary reconstruction of the atrium.

HOME SWEET HOME!

While the Forum, the baths, the theatres, the amphitheatre and the inns were the centre of the Romans' intense municipal life, the domus, i.e. the house, was looked upon as a 'refuge' and the heart of the family's private life. The town plan of Pompeii is characterized by a web of streets which cross one another to form a number of blocks called 'insulae'. The houses were built on these insulae and the area corresponding to one insula usually comprised several independent houses, but there were also important residences such as the House of the Faun which occupied a whole block.

Generally speaking, the residential buildings in Pompeii are one-family houses with no upper floor and are completely 'sealed off' from their surroundings. Their rooms are arranged in a hierarchical pattern round a central courtyard called the atrium. The house was lit through an opening in the roof of the atrium called the compluvium. The rainwater was collected in a pool called the impluvium, positioned right under the compluvium, and from there it was made to flow into an underlying cistern where it was stored.

A narrow hallway called the fauces provided access to the house which was often flanked by tabernae (shops) opening directly onto the street.

The atrium is an inner courtyard open to the sky. When the surrounding roof has no supporting pillars, the atrium is said to be of the Tuscan type, if it has four supporting pillars it is called a tetrastyle

Imaginary reconstruction of the atrium of a Pompeian house.

Imaginary reconstruction of houses and shops along Via dell'Abbondanza.

atrium, and if there are more than four pillars it is said to be of the Corinthian type. A number of smaller rooms, usually cubicula (bedrooms) or storerooms, were situated on either side of the atrium. The tablinum was usually positioned opposite the main door and was both the most important and the most 'sacred' part of the house, being used both for reception purposes and as the hub of family life. The family's archives and the images of its forefathers were kept in the alae - two rooms positioned on either side of the atrium. The larger houses had a back garden which could be reached through a hallway from the atrium and was mainly used to grow

vegetables to meet the needs of the family.

In the 2" century B.C. the average size of the house increased as a result of the influence of Hellenistic construction techniques. In place of the vegetable garden the Romans began to build a peristyle, i.e. a colonnade, and would decorate the garden with sculptures and fountains and arrange the remaining living rooms all around it.

For less pretentious houses they would occasionally depart from the classical model with the rooms all around the atrium and adopt a different plan. The rooms were positioned along a longitudinal axis starting from the entrance and were arranged on either side of a rectangular room without an impluvium - respectively facing the inner garden and the street. This type of house usually had an upper floor whose rooms opened onto a landing at the top of a wooden staircase.

THE SUBSEQUENT STAGES IN THE CONSTRUCTION OF THE TOWN

It stands to the credit of the archaeologist Amedeo Maiuri, who is universally acclaimed as the greatest specialist in Pompeian history, that his identification of a number of successive stages in the construction of the town of Pompeii has been acknowledged and confirmed by many other archaeologists and scholars:

Pre-Samnite Age *(tuff-stone and sandstone, opus quadratum)*, 6th-5th centuries B.C..

First Samnite Age *(sandstone and volcanic material: opus quadratum and opus incertum)*, 4th-3rd centuries B.C.

Second Samnite Age *(tuff-stone buildings with Hellenistic influences)*, 200-80 B.C.

First Period of the Roman Colony - Republican and Augustan Ages *(opus saccarium, opus quasi-reticulatum and opus reticulatum)* 80 B.C. - 14 A.D.

Second Period of the Roman Colony - Age of Claudius and first Age of Flavius *(opus mixtum and bricks)* A.D. 14-79.

Another type of Pompeian building is the one used simultaneously for residential and commercial purposes. In this kind of house the ground-floor usually comprised a shop looking onto the street and a back-room and was possibly completed by one or two upper floors.

In the 2" century B.C., houses were built in the part of the town which commands a scenic view of the countryside as far as the sea. Some of the houses were built right upon the town walls so as to conceal the latter from sight, while others were constructed by terracing the natural slopes of the hill on which the original core of the town had been founded.

As it is unlikely that the town was ever overpopulated, it hardly experiencied any of the problems associated with the shortage of housing. In Rome and Ostia such problems led to the emergence of a new multi-storey building divided into several apartments, each of which could be reached from the street via an independent stairway. In the 2" century, when the more affluent families of the town felt the need for more luxurious dwellings, they began to build themselves villas outside the town. These were so large that they exceeded the limits of a single insula and were designed according to architectural principles intended to establish a close relationship between the building and its natural surroundings. They were usually divided into a residential section proper and a rural section which was used in the running of farming activities.

The fresco of Priapus weighing his enormous phallus at the entrance to the house. This was considered to be a propitiatory symbol of wealth.

The peristyle of the House of the Vettii; the garden was embellished with statuettes, columns and fountains. Today it has been partly reconstructed.

24 THE HOUSE OF THE VETTII **

This luxurious residence houses an impressive collection of fresco decorations typical of the wall paintings in the houses of rich Pompeian traders. The excavation techniques used made it possible to preserve, in almost all the rooms in the complex, the fourth-style figure paintings completed after the earthquake of 62 A.D.. The brothers Aulus Vettius Restitutus and Aulus Vettius Conviva commissioned their fresco decorations from one of the leading artists' workshops so that their home would be not only a comfortable residence but also a 'status symbol'. The house is divided into two areas: firstly, the part in which the family lived, laid out around the main atrium and the peristyle with its beautiful garden (this house does not have the tablinum which was traditionally built between the two, opposite the main entrance); and secondly, the part where the servants lived and worked, on the right of the entrance hall and centred around a small atrium with a lararium. The wall facing the entrance (1) is decorated with a fresco of Priapus weighing his phallus on a pair of scales and a sheep with the attributes of Mercury, the god of financial income, which here serve to protect the house from bad luck and as propitiatory symbols of wealth. The atrium (3) is decorated with scenes depicting sacrifices, hunts and cupids while two strong-boxes are anchored to stone blocks in the floor. The decision to site them here can probably be explained by the desire of the masters of the house to underline their wealth and importance. The rooms laid out on the left of the entrance hall are decorated

with mythological subjects, which are described below. On the right-hand wall in the first room (4) we can see a fresco depicting the **myth of Leander** swimming towards his beloved Hero, while the opposite wall portrays **Ariadne abandoned by Theseus** on Naxos. The next room (5) is decorated with frescoes depicting the **struggle between Cupid and Pan**, **Cyparissus** who is transformed into a cypress tree after killing a sacred stag and, lastly, some images of Jupiter in the upper section of the wall. The two rooms (alae) (6-7) opening off the

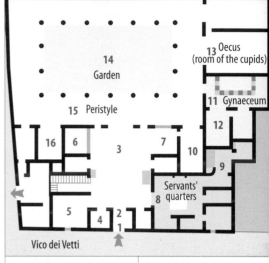

1 Vestibulum	10 Triclinium (room of Ixion)
2 Fauces	11 Gynaeceum
3 Atrium	12 Triclinium
4 Cubiculum	13 Oecus (room of the cupids)
5 Oecus	14 Garden
6-7 Alae	15 Peristyle
8 Servants' quarters	16 Oecus (room of Pentheus)
9 Kitchen	

The lararium
of the servants' quarters.

Imaginary reconstruction
of the perystile and garden.

A room (7) with decorations on a background painted in yellow. Below: the room named after Ixion.

atrium just before it leads into the garden have frescoes painted on a yellow background; these depict a cock fight on the left, and two medallions portraying the heads of Medusa and Silenus on the right. The peristyle (15) is decorated with black panelling with alternate still life and figure paintings. The garden (14) has been mostly rebuilt according to its original layout and was lavishly decorated with bronze and marble statuettes of cherubs and cupids, busts and heads on columns, tables, rectangular marble fountains along the four sides and round fountains in the four corners and in the centre. Along the side of the peristyle facing the atrium we find two reception rooms that open onto the garden and are lavishly decorated with frescoes of mythological scenes set inside painted aediculae.

The living room on the left (16) just beyond the atrium has yellow painted walls with frescoes depicting: on the left, **Hercules strangling the serpents** sent by Juno; on the right **the punishment of Dirce** bound to the horns of a raging bull by Amphion and Zetus; while in the centre we see **the suffering of Pentheus** torn limb from limb by the Bacchantes. The living room on the right (10) just beyond the atrium is decorated with a lower section of imitation coloured marble while, amidst an architectural flight of fancy, we can see: on the left, **Daedalus** presenting **Pasiphae** with the wooden cow in which she would hide as she was in love with a bull, and from whose union she was to give birth to the Minotaur; in the centre, the punishment inflicted on **Ixion** who is tied to a wheel built by Hephaestus and made to turn for all eternity as Hera sitting on the throne and Hermes look on; on the right, we can see **Bacchus watching Ariadne as she sleeps** on a tiger skin. Leaving the living room and following the peristyle we find a few rooms set to one side and thought to have been reserved for women (gynaeceum) (11), where we can see a triclinium (12) and a cubiculum opposite a small garden.

Two frescoes in this area depict **Odysseus recognising Achilles**, and **Auge surprised by a drunken Hercules**. The triclinium (13) runs in the same direction as the garden (which has been planted with the original aromatic herbs) and houses an extremely unusual miniaturised decoration above a lower panel. This portrays **cupids** and their female equivalents (psyches) engaged in a number of different activities; from right to left these scenes depict:

The House of the Vettii is lavishly decorated with wonderful paintings.

An erotic scene.

The room of the cupids is decorated with figures standing out against a red background.

archery; arranging flowers and making floral crowns with roses carried by a billy goat; the manufacture and sale of perfumes; races with chariots drawn by antelopes; a goldsmith's workshop; work in a dyer's shop.

On the rear wall we can see, again from right to left: bakers celebrating their tutelary god Vesta; winemaking; the triumphal procession of Bacchus lying on a cart pulled by billy-goats; the sale of wine.

The figure paintings which were here fastened to the wall by nails are now missing while the vermillion side panels depict well-known divine couples in flight. From the right, **Perseus and Andromeda**, **Dionysus and Ariadne**, **Apollo and Daphne**, **Neptune and Amymone** and, beside the entrance, **Silenus astonished by Hermaphroditos**.

Leaving the residential part of the house through a doorway beside the main entrance, we come into the area where the servants worked and lived.

In the small atrium (8) we find the lararium, the altar to the domestic gods, on which we can see a scene depicting the Genius with two Lares dancing on either side above a serpent, the symbol of regenerative power.

In the fireplace in the kitchen (9) we can see some tripods with 5 bronze pans and other containers, while in the adjoining room, which was reserved for the cook and was decorated with erotic paintings, we find a marble statue of Priapus that had originally been used as a fountain in the garden.

The triclinium which runs in the same direction as the garden houses miniaturised decorations depicxting cupids and their female equivalents (psyches) engaged in a number of different activities.

PAINTINGS TO INSPIRE DREAMS

The wall decorations in Roman houses and villas have been subdivided into four styles according to figural content and chronology.

The **First Style**, also called 'encrustation style', was popular from 150 B.C. up to 80 B.C. and can be recognised by the shiny stucco decoration imitating marble-lined walls. The final result is achieved by inserting a variety of colours into different partitions for the lower panel, for the smooth paintings and for the rusticated paintings.

The **Second Style**, also referred to as the 'architectural style', is characterised by the fact that for the first time the walls of the house create an illusion of being 'open' to the outside world. This style was common between 80 B.C. and 14 A.D. and involved the depiction of architectures which extended the physical space of the house towards imaginary landscapes. The decoration does not merely at-

1ˢᵗ style painting. The House of Sallust.

2ⁿᵈ style painting. The Villa of Mysteries.

tempt to imitate marble patterns but makes good use of perspective to create two or more levels of depth. These compositions included columns in the foreground and colonnades in perspective disappearing into the distance with figure subjects or large paintings depicting a mythological, heroic or religious theme, in addition to small panels with doors set between the architectural features. This highly scenographic decoration seems to have been inspired by a growing theatrical taste.

The **Third Style**, up to the year 62 A.D., abandons the use of space and architectural features as the subject matter of the composition with the result that the overall decoration loses depth. The columns, balustrades, architraves and shelves are flattened against the wall to conserve a purely ornamental function. Columns are often used in an elongated form to frame large figure paintings inserted in large areas of plain-coloured wall.

Landscapes are reduced to miniatures inserted into a single colour background, now painted in new shades of sea-green and golden yellow.

The Third Style is also referred to as 'pseudo-Egyptian' because of the presence of typically Egyptian elements: lotus flowers, small stars, rosettes, coloured fillets and a band running above the skirting with details of still life scenes, gardens with bullrushes and elegant birds in a variety of poses. The wall decorations depicting large-scale subjects inspired by gardens with trees, fountains, pools, small columns and birds in flight also belong to this period.

From the earthquake of 62 A.D. up to the town's destruction in 79 A.D., the houses in Pompeii were decorated with **Fourth Style** paintings. These were also said to be in the 'ornamental style' because the whole wall is treated simply as a free ornamental composition. The architectural features no longer have any reference to reality and are reduced to unreal designs, a mere flight of fancy in which ornamentation is often excessive. There is also frequent

The Fourth Style was a sign of wealth that typified the houses of the rich merchants of Pompeii before the catastrophe. Several experts believe that this tendency drew inspiration from the models adopted in the Domus Aurea, the imperial palace in Rome, built after Nero had set fire to the capital in 64 A.D. destroying many buildings. Fufidius Successus with his workshop in Via Castrice was the best known painter in Pompeii. The frescoes decorating the houses are not signed by the artist as the work was completed by more than one person, often working in series. However, experts can recognise the work of the individual groups of artists through their representation of certain details.

The wall paintings in Pompeii were executed using the 'fresco' technique, by which the basic outline of the composition was prepared and the colours were then added to the fresh plaster so that, by penetrating inwards, the overall painting would last longer. This greater resistance to the effects of time and wear is due to the protection of a transparent film of calcium carbonate that is formed by the reaction between the slaked lime in the plaster and the air.

This natural protection forced painters to use the encaustic technique only to fix the expensive red colour, basically obtained from mercury and known as cinnabar red, which gave a brighter shade of red than the one obtained with an ochre base.

When the actual painting was finished a fine layer of wax was passed over the work.

use of bas-relief stucco work, as in the Second Style. Figure paintings become smaller or disappear altogether. Formal subjects are chosen, often inspired by philosophical or exotic themes, although we still find paintings that draw on the everyday life or news reports of important events, such as the brawl that took place in the Amphitheatre, the painting of which is now displayed at the National Archaeological Museum in Naples.

3rd style painting.
The House of Marcus Lucretius Fronto.

4th style painting.
The House of Fabius Rufus.

Detail of a winged figure.

25 THE HOUSE OF THE ANCIENT HUNT ✳

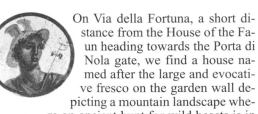

On Via della Fortuna, a short distance from the House of the Faun heading towards the Porta di Nola gate, we find a house named after the large and evocative fresco on the garden wall depicting a mountain landscape where an ancient hunt for wild beasts is in progress. It is a house of Samnite origin and contains some fine examples of fourth style decoration. Personifications of autumn and winter are depicted on the walls of the atrium, while the facing walls of the second cubiculum on the right portray mythological subjects. On the left we can see **Leda and the swan**, portrayed amid medallions with the busts of Jupiter and Diana and, on the right, **Venus fishing** between Mercury and Apollo. In the tablinum we find Nile landscapes with Pygmies, cherubs hunting wild beasts and a highly effective depiction of carpets and pieces of cloth billowing in the wind. The exedra opposite the garden is embellished with fantastic architectures and lavish ornamental motifs in which we can see **Diana bathing as Actaeon watches**, and **Apollo** in the background **with a shepherd**.

The tablinum.

*The tablinum:
small pictures portraying scenes of cherubs
hunting wild beasts.*

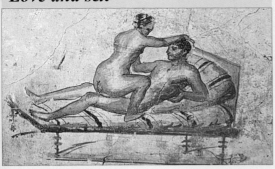

UNINHIBITED EROS

Love was a common topic of conversation in Pompeii. Feelings, passions, poetic love, sex, homosexuality, prostitution and so forth were all part of daily life and not a source of prejudice. The concept of 'obscenity' seems to have been unknown. Love and sex were considered earthly practices of a man's life that were encouraged by the benevolence of Venus. The thousands of examples of graffiti found on the town's walls are unequivocal proof of what the people of Pompeii thought about love and sex. Pompeii was thus held to be the town of Venus, the goddess of love and the regenerative force in nature to whom Silla dedicated the colony. We therefore find several places of cult worship dedicated to the goddess, and she is also the subject of many paintings and poetic graffiti found scratched into the walls, Venus was deeply rooted in the life of every Pompeian and no one seemed to want to hide this.

In the Basilica we find clear proof of this in an inscription: "If you are looking for sweet embraces in

Opinions about the women of Pompeii

What did the men who lived in Pompeii up to 79 A.D. think of the town's women? Their 'opinions' are expressed in the many examples of graffiti found scratched in the walls.
"You are Venus", writes one man before the name of his partner; and another states "If you have not seen the portrait of Venus by Apelles, look at my girlfriend, she's just as beautiful as her". There are also numerous sensual comments, such as "... may you thus always be in flower, oh Sabina, and maintain your good looks for ever". Among the graffiti we also find admiration for women of more doubtful virtues: "Beautiful girl", writes one lover who is aware that he shares his girlfriend with others, "for Ceius and many more". The walls of Pompeii are literally full of comments inspired by the Roman poets. "Love moves me", writes one "now that I write and Cupid guides my hand: may I die if I choose to be a god, without you by my side.".

this town, you will find that all the girls here are available".

The town had numerous brothels, or 'lupanares', with young women from every part of the empire, each one specialised in a particular sexual technique. Rooms for sexual encounters were also to be found in many taverns, baths and even ordinary houses which sometimes had rooms decorated with erotic frescoes for the sexual entertainment of guests.

The use of phallic symbols in frescoes, sculptures, charms, lamps, and in many corners of the town's houses, on the facades of the buildings and at the entrance to shops was very common. Surprisingly, these actually referred to magical practices as the phallus was considered the primordial positive force in nature and, thus, the main and most effective amulet against the evil eye and a sure way of ensuring health and well-being.

26 THE LUPANAR (BROTHEL) **

The Lupanar was the official brothel of Pompeii. As a trading town, it was visited every day by large numbers of people, especially traders from other towns. The brothel is situated at the intersection of two side roads on Via dell'Abbondanza near the town centre, not far from the Forum and the Stabian Baths (which had a rear entrance on the Vicolo del Lupanare). Phalluses engraved on the basalt road surface or on stones set into the facades of houses gave visitors clear indications on how to reach the brothel. We find explicit reference to the use to which this building was put, unlike many other brothels in the town (there were probably 25 in all) which were situated on the first floor above taverns and houses. The lupanar had ten stone beds with mattresses, each bed set in its own small room. Five of these were found on the ground floor, while the larger rooms were situated on the first floor which could be reached by an independent entrance and a wooden staircase. The customers expressed their opinions on the brothel and the performance of the prostitutes by scratching them on the walls, as can be seen by the approximately 120 examples of explicit graffiti. The brothel was managed by a 'leno' (an owner of prostitutes) who bought the girls as slaves, primarily in the East, at an average price of 600 sesterces. The brothel's tariffs varied from 2 to 16 asses (1 as was equal to about half a sesterce).

To the right of the entrance on the ground floor, the wall has a painting of Priapus depicted with two phalluses, one in each hand, while on the doors to the rooms we find illustrated scenes of sexual acts advertising the 'specialities' of the resident prostitutes.

Aerial view of the Theatres.

Itinerary 3

THE THEATRE DISTRICT

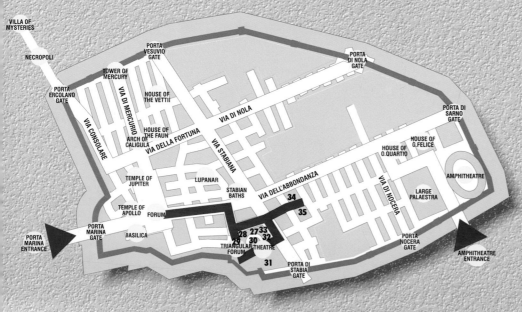

27   **TEMPLE OF ISIS**
28   **SAMNITE GYMNASIUM**
29   * **TRIANGULAR FORUM**
30 ** **LARGE THEATRE**
31   * **GLADIATORS' BARRACKS**
32 ** **ODEION**
33   **TEMPLE OF JUPITER MEILICHIOS**
34   * **HOUSE OF THE CEII**
35   * **HOUSE OF MENANDER**

* worth seeing
** not to be missed

View of the Temple of Isis.

Just behind the Large Theatre we find the Temple of Isis with its entrance in the street of the same name (Via del Tempio di Iside). Originally dating from between the late 2" and early 1" centuries B.C., it was totally rebuilt after the earthquake of 62 A.D. at the expense of an ex-slave (libertus) who had since made his fortune. As he could not himself enter the Council of Decurions he had the work carried out in the name of his six-year-old son, as is explained in an inscription on the entrance to the temple: "Numerius Popidius Celsinus, son of Numerius, at his own expense entirely rebuilt the Temple of Isis which had collapsed during the earthquake. In view of such generosity the decurions admitted him to their assembly free of char-

Statue of Isis.

Imaginary reconstruction of the Temple of Isis.

ge, even though he was only six years old". The cult of Isis became fairly widespread during the Hellenistic era due to the religious links the Greeks had with Egypt and the Orient, and it had a particularly large following in Pompeii as the town had strong trading ties with the East. The temple stands on a tall podium situated in the centre of a porticoed courtyard. The cella, which is greater in width than in length and can be reached by means of a stone stairway to one side, is situated behind a portico with four columns to the front and two niches for statues of divinities from the cult of Isis.

Behind the temple there is a large meeting room which was probably used during preparations for the rites. Excavation work between the entrance columns unearthed a marble hand, a golden goblet, a statuette, two bronze candlesticks and two human skulls, which were probably used in cult rituals. To the sides of the room there are two other rooms which were obviously connected with the cult as four wooden statues with marble heads, hands and feet were found in one of them. In front of the temple in the left-hand corner of the portico we find a room that was designated for purification ceremonies (purgatorium) where water from the river Nile was kept in containers in the basement underneath. The main altar is situated between the temple and the purgatorium, while the others are generally located between the columns. All the finds from the temple as well as the decorations removed from the walls are exhibited in the National Archaeological Museum in Naples.

High Priest of Isis, now exhibited in the
National Archaeological Museum in Naples.

28 SAMNITE GYMNASIUM

The discovery of a statue of Doriphorus, the symbol of youth and strength and a Roman copy of the original by Polycletus, led early archaeologists to define this space with its surrounding colonnades beside the Large Theatre as a gymnasium (palaestra). However, it was actually the headquarters of a military association of noble Pompeian youths who used to train here for parades and official competitions. The limited space available meant that certain kinds of training probably took place in the adjoining area of the Triangular Forum. The building dates back to the 2" century B.C. and is enclosed by tuff-stone Doric columns on three sides only as, after the earthquake of 62 A.D., the nearby Temple of Isis was extended into the gymnasium area. Opposite the entrance there are two pedestals, the larger of which most probably housed the statue of Doriphorus. Beside it was a flight of steps which allowed the young athletes to place crowns on the statue. The lower pedestal was used for placing gifts.

The marble statue of Doriphorus, currently in the N. Archaeological Museum in Naples.

The courtyard of the Samnite Gymnasium.

FROM THE PHALLUS TO ISIS

It is a recurring feature of human history - and Pompeii was no exception - that man's religious practices have been a mixture of both public and private devotion and superstition, and have often reached ridiculous levels of symbolism in order to ward off bad luck or the evil eye.

The ancient cults of the local inhabitants, which were generally linked to the rituals of nature and fertility, later gave way to the worship of Hercules, Bacchus and Venus, the chosen 'patrons' of Pompeii.

In Pompeii, Venus was worshipped as the creator of the universe since it was she who meted out life and death; she was the Venus of Pompeii (Venus Pompeiana) and also mother nature (Venus Physica) and the goddess of fertility and abundance.

A temple was erected in honour of the goddess on the promontory which could be seen from the sea, and many images of her were displayed around the town. Other popular cults included that of Apollo (the main god worshipped in Pompeii in the 6th cen-

Bronze pendant with a large phallus 'used' as an amulet.

Via dell'Abbondanza. The Venus of Pompeii amid flying cupids

tury B.C.) and the cult of the Capitoline triad of Jupiter, Juno and Minerva, whose temple, or Capitolium, stood to the north of the Forum. The Pompeians also honoured the divinities who watched over the goods which were transported by sea and along the river Sarno. Outside Pompeii, near the town's river port, a sanctuary was erected to Neptune and a votive shrine was found there along with an inscription.

Of course, the cult of the Emperor was also widespread, and in particular his 'Genius' and his 'Fortune' were revered. A private citizen erected the Temple of Fortuna Augusta at his own expense near the Forum, while a temple was built and dedicated to the 'Genius of Vespasian' in a small area of the Forum itself. Nearby, a Temple to the Public Lares was built, probably after the earthquake of 62 A.D.. It was dedicated to the protectors of the town in order to regain their goodwill and placate their anger as, according to popular belief, this had been responsible for the terrible calamity.

Frequent contact with the East led to the importation of rites involving orgies, which were dedicated in particular to Isis. A temple was erected to the Egyptian goddess in the theatre district and several houses in Pompeii bear witness to her cult. In the so-called House of Magical Rites, dedicated to the god Sabatius, some interesting finds include two

Mercury in a small Etruscan-style temple

res, to whom an altar was also dedicated.

The tutelary deities of the house were originally the spirits of the ancestors who in various paintings were often accompanied by the 'Geniuses', i.e. the symbols of the procreating strength of the head of each family.

The most popular simulacra of the town's divinities can be seen in some of the paintings discovered here, but they were more often represented in bronzes placed on altar shelves. Libations were frequently offered to them during meals in order to obtain their favour.

The roots of Pompeian religious beliefs basically lay in superstition. Practices against the evil eye and every kind of disease in favour of health, fertility and love were very common, as is indicated by the various amulets discovered around the town. The most popular amulet among the Pompeians was the phallus. It was reproduced in every possible manner, from paintings and bas-reliefs to pendants, and could be found everywhere: on the walls of houses, at the entrances to shops, on fountains and even inside houses.

Bacchus and Mount Vesuvius from the House of the Centenary.

bronze 'magic hands' and two sacrificial vases. Lastly, evidence of the cult of the 'Magna Mater', the great goddess Cybele or the 'Great mother of the Gods' who was associated with fertility and fecundity, can be seen in popular paintings such as those in a felt-makers' shop in Via dell'Abbondanza. Oriental cults enjoyed a considerable following since they professed theories of salvation by promising a better after-life.

In any house the religious nature of the inhabitants of Pompeii was clearly visible in the cult of the La-

The procession of Cybele and the god Dionysus in the niche.

Via dell'Abbondanza. Bas-relief depicting the phallus in a small temple.

View of the base of the
Doric temple.

The temple (possibly
no more than a sacellum
after the temple was
abandoned) was used for
athletic games and
displays and also as a
space for the public
during the intervals of
theatrical performances.

Here below and facing
page: reconstructions
of the Triangular Forum.

This building is clearly visible from the sea as it is situated on the promontory of the hill of Pompeii and commands a wide view over the plain below. Passing along Via dell'Abbondanza to the end of Via dei Teatri we find a portico with three Ionic columns and a semicolumn which form the entrance to the Triangular Forum. The Hellenistic style arrangement of the area, which has a colonnade with 95 columns, dates back to the 2nd century B.C.. This intervention created a harmonious protective curtain around the pre-existing Doric Temple and at the same time annexed this sacred area to the theatre district and the two gymnasiums as the four-sided portico behind the stage of the Theatre was connected to the Triangular Forum by means of a stairway. Three openings along the eastern portico connected it to the far hemicycle of the Large Theatre and the Samnite Gymnasium. The Doric Temple was built using limestone from the Sarno valley during the mid 6th century B.C. and was dedicated to Hercules, although it was later also adopted for the cult of Minerva. However, it was abandoned some time before the destruction of Pompeii. The monument had seven Doric columns along its shorter sides and eleven along the longer ones. At the foot of the steps leading up to the temple there is a tomb-like structure which was probably a monument erected to the cult of the founder of the town. In front of the remains of the temple there are three pre-Roman tuff-stone altars and a well surrounded by a circular building with Doric columns, while at the rear we find a semicircular tuff-stone seat which enjoys an uninterrupted view of the Gulf of Naples.

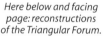
POMPEI · ANTIQVI ·
TEMPLVM · GRAECVM ·
FORVM · TRIANGVLARE ·
DOMVS · QVATVOR · TABVLATORVM ·

POMPEI · ANTIQVI ·
TEMPLVM · GRAECVM ·
FORVM · TRIANGVLARE ·
OPPIDVM

Letters indicating the place reserved for Marcus Holconius Rufus, duumvir of Pompeii, who with his brother financed the extension work to the theatre.

Layout
of the Theatres and
the Triangular Forum

1   Temple of Isis
2   Samnite Gymnasium
3   Triangular Forum
4   Doric Temple
5   Tholos
6   Gladiators' Barracks
7   Large Theatre
8   Odeion
9   Temple of Jupiter
    Meilichios

③⓪ THE LARGE THEATRE ✱✱

Although it is actually the only theatre in Pompeii it was given this name to distinguish it from the nearby Odeion, which is much smaller and was used for different purposes. It was built in the 2" century B.C. more or less according to traditional Greek canons in so far as the tiered seating makes use of a natural slope and the orchestra is arranged in a horse-shoe shape.

It was extended and restored during the reign of Augustus at the personal expense of the Holconius brothers, who were rich Pompeian vine growers. An inscription tells us that the entire seating area had been resurfaced in marble, but this was removed and carried off after the destruction of the town. The upper circle was added to increase the seating capacity and the two side boxes built above the entrances to the orchestra were reserved for the guests of honour.

In this way the theatre of Pompeii could accommodate 5,000 people seated in three different areas which were separated by corridors. The first (called the ima cavea) was situated in the orchestra itself and had four rows of seats which were reserved for the decurions, while the first rows of the media cavea were for the representatives of the corporations: one of these was reserved for the eldest of the Holconius brothers and was identified by an inscription in bronze letters. The remaining places right up to the top part (summa cavea) were designated for the ordinary townspeople. The final tier had stone rings fitted into the walls which were used to support the poles which held the large canopy covering the theatre to protect the audience from the sun.

The stone stage was rebuilt after the earthquake of 62 A.D. in imitation of the facade of an important building decorated with columns, niches and statues. To the rear was a small and unusual-shaped dressing room running the whole width of the stage area, which could be reached by three doors directly from the stage. A further three doors lead out onto a large courtyard.

③① THE GLADIATORS' BARRACKS

In the latter years of Pompeii the four-sided colonnade rising up behind the Theatre was used as the barracks of the organisation of gladiators who performed in the town.

Along the wings of the colonnade and on the first floor were the rooms which provided accommodation for the gladiators from other towns. Paraments, helmets and arms belonging to the gladiators were found in many of the rooms.

The four-sided colonnade with its 74 Doric columns was originally used as an extension of the theatre: for example, the public could go there for something to eat (performances often lasted most of the day) or to take shelter from the rain.

It is likely that for a few years this space was used both by the theatre and as the headquarters of an organisation responsible for the sporting, intellectual and military training of the town's youth.

Colonnade of the Gladiators' Barracks.

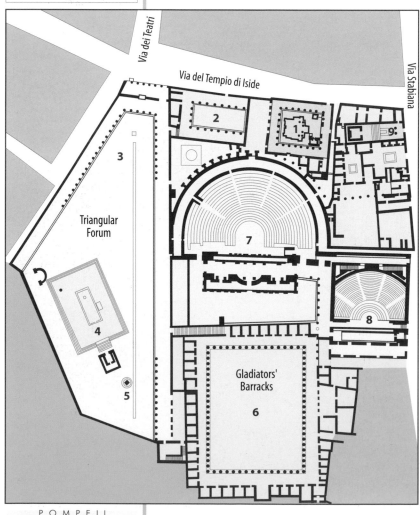

Gladiator helmets.

The large courtyard of the Gladiators' Barracks.

The tiered seating and the stage of the Large Theatre.

On the top of the tiered seating there are two unusual tuff-stone figures of telamons in a kneeling position and holding a shelf with decorative elements.

32 THE ODEION ✱✱

This covered theatre situated near the Large Theatre was mainly used for concerts, although it also was also the chosen venue for poetry recitals. It was built by the same two duumviri responsible for the construction of the Amphitheatre during the early years of the Roman colony in an area which had originally been developed by the Samnites. The tiered seating was cut away to one side to allow the construction of a perimeter wall designed to support the four-sided roof. The first seats in front of the orchestra hemicycle, which was paved with slabs of coloured marble chips, were reserved for the decurions and were laid out on top of four rows of wide tuff-stone steps. The tiered seating was served by semicircular steps to the sides of the orchestra. Boxes for the guests of honour were situated on either side of the stage area from which they could be reached, while three doors in the stage wall opened onto the backstage dressing room and from here led directly outside.

Entrance to the Odeion on Via Stabiana.

33 THE TEMPLE OF JUPITER MEILICHIOS

The name of the temple was discovered thanks to an inscription in the Oscan language found on the Porta di Stabia gate. This cult enjoyed a particular following in Pompeii due to trade links with Magna Grecia, where it was fairly widespread. A Nucerian tuff-stone altar stands in the courtyard and dates back to between the 3rd and 2" centuries B.C.. The temple itself stands on a tall podium with four Corinthian columns at the front and two at the sides, behind which was the cella where terra-cotta statues of Jupiter and Juno and a bust of Minerva were found.

The discovery of the divinities of the Capitoline triad, who were worshipped in the Capitolium in the Forum, suggests that the cult had been temporarily transferred here after the earthquake of 62 A.D. while restoration work was being carried out on the main temple.

View of the temple. The name 'meilichios' given to Jupiter - to whom this temple in Via Stabiana (near the Odeion) is dedicated - literally means 'sweet as honey'.

A statue of Jupiter Meilichios on display at the Archaeological Museum in Naples

Imaginary reconstruction of the Temple of Jupiter Meilichios.

The tetrastyle atrium of the house of the Ceii.

34 THE HOUSE OF THE CEII ✳

This small house stands opposite the well-known House of Menander in Vicolo Meridionale, which can be reached directly from Via Stabiana by taking the side street almost opposite the Temple of Jupiter Meilichios. The name was given to the house by the archaeologists who chose it from one of the nine election slogans painted on the front wall. The rooms are decorated with original third style paintings: in the winter triclinium, to the right of the four-columned atrium with its fountain in the impluvium, we see a young Bacchus offering wine to a tiger; in the next room, adjacent to the garden, there are paintings of busts of satyrs and maenads. The decorations on the three walls of the garden are particularly striking. They depict landscapes with pseudo-Egyptian motifs and scenes of wild beasts hunting: wolves chasing wild boars, a tiger chasing two rams and a lion pursuing a bull. There is also a Nile landscape depicting pygmies struggling with a hippopotamus and a crocodile.

A detail from the hunting scene painted on the front wall of the garden.

35 THE HOUSE OF MENANDER ✳✳

The name derives from the fresco of the poet Menander, discovered in a room behind the peristyle.

The house belonged to Quintus Poppaeus, one of the Poppaeus family to whom Nero's second wife, Poppaea Sabina, most probably belonged.
It extends over 2,000 square metres and reflects the traditional layout of a Roman house, with its atrium and peristyle as well as servants quarters and a bath-house. Before admiring the large peristyle it is worth stopping briefly in the atrium, where the lararium is situated in the right-hand corner, and in the room to the left (opposite the impluvium) where the walls are frescoed with a triptych inspired by the Trojan war. On the right we can see the death of Laocoon who, along with his children, was strangled by a snake; to the right, Cassandra resists abduction by Odysseus and lastly, in the centre, Cassandra tries to convince the Trojans not to let the wooden horse enter the city. The floor of the living room in the peristyle in the right-hand corner just past the tablinum is of particular interest as it

One side of the peristyle containing the niches.

contains a charming mosaic in the centre depicting a scene with pygmies rowing a boat on the river Nile. On the walls decorated with a fourth style green background there are also scenes of Centaurs abducting the Lapithae women. A corridor opening to the right of the peristyle leads to the kitchens, several basement areas and the vegetable garden.

In this area a box was discovered containing 118 items of silverware, some gold objects and a few coins, all of which had been stored away until restoration work on the house was completed.

On returning to the peristyle we find the bathhouse whose calidarium still has its original mosaic floor and painted stucco wall decorations.

There are four niches at the rear of the peristyle, two of which are rectangular while the others are apsidal. The first one on the right is decorated with second style paintings and has an altar dedicated to the cult of the Lares, which were originally represented by five wooden or wax sculptures from which the plaster casts seen here were made.

Next to an apsidal niche there is a rectangular one with an illustration on the right-hand wall of the poet Menander seated. Just before the corner of the peristyle there is a cubiculum which was originally a double bedroom.

The position of the mosaic floor would seem to confirm this, even though it has also been suggested that it was used as a storeroom where books were kept on four shelves. Beyond this area we find the part of the house where the servants lived and worked, with cells for the slaves, storerooms for wine and stables.

After the main peristyle there is a large triclinium where some of the walls of the previous construction have been dug up. In the living room which opens out on the right we find the plaster casts of the bodies of twelve treasure-hunting thieves who had come here following the catastrophe of 79 A.D. with the intention of stripping the house of its valuable objects.

Cassandra resisting abduction by Odysseus, one of the paintings from the triptych inspired by the Trojan war.

Detail of a mosaic floor depicting scenes of pygmies on the river Nile.

The atrium of the house.

The plaster casts of the wooden or wax statues of the Lares.

THE FOUNTAINS

The town of Pompeii contained a wealth of public fountains. The pictures illustrate a sequence of highly original subjects whose decorations were carved from blocks of marble or lava stone.

THE STREETS

The streets of Pompeii vary in width from 2.5 to 4.5 metres and are made from large slabs of Vesuvian lava, while the pavements, which are usually around 30 centimetres high, were surfaced with a mixture of broken terra-cotta and fat lime cement, most of which has been worn away by the millions of visitors. One interesting feature is the so-called 'pedestrian crossings', made from stone slabs of equal height to the pavement, placed across the street. These allowed pedestrians to cross the road without getting their feet wet or dirty as the streets were often filthy due to the lack of a proper sewer network.

However, the slabs were placed in such a way that carts could still pass, as can be seen by the ruts left in the road by the cart-wheels.

In keeping with the definitions given to the street layout of Greek cities, in Pompeii the term 'decumanus' used to describe the main streets running from west to east and 'cardo' for the streets generally running from north to south to connect up the various decumani.

Via Stabiana.

The Villa of Misteries.

Itinerary 4

FROM THE FORUM TO THE VILLA OF MYSTERIES

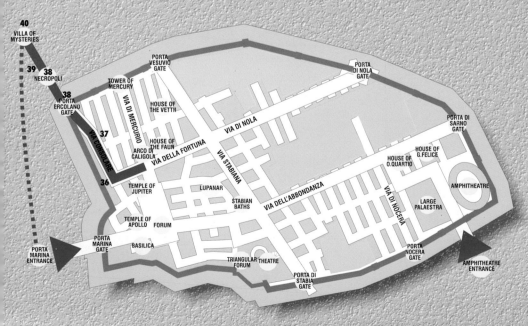

36 **HOUSE OF FABIUS RUFUS**
37 * **HOUSE OF SALLUST**
38 * **PORTA ERCOLANO GATE AND NECROPOLIS**
39 * **VILLA OF DIOMEDES**
40 ** **VILLA OF MYSTERIES**

  * *worth seeing*
 ** *not to be missed*

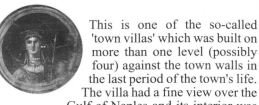

This is one of the so-called 'town villas' which was built on more than one level (possibly four) against the town walls in the last period of the town's life. The villa had a fine view over the Gulf of Naples and its interior was entirely decorated in the Pompeian fourth style. The villa itself is the result of the fusion of a number of previously built houses and so, in a tiny room in the central apsidal structure, we can find the remains of second style frescoes, including what appears to be a portrait of the Venus of Pompeii. The side walls in the same area are also decorated with stars and small moon designs, suggesting that the room may have been used for astrology.

A second style fresco portraying the Venus of Pompeii.

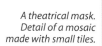

A theatrical mask. Detail of a mosaic made with small tiles.

A living room decorated with fourth-style frescoes.

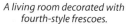

Small painting of a mythological theme.

37 THE HOUSE OF SALLUST *

This house, which is situated in the town's western quarter just before the street forks to the left towards the Porta Ercolano gate, is one of the oldest in Pompeii, dating from the 3rd century B.C..
In addition to the atrium with its surrounding rooms, it has a small covered porch behind the tablinum, a garden and a summer triclinium with stone couches.

Towards the rear of the building there is a kitchen, a dining room and several bedrooms.
The front of the building houses four shops, a tavern and a bakery with three millstones and an oven with a fireplace alongside.
The owner probably took advantage of the house's proximity to the Porta Ercolano gate and converted it into a boarding house with a number of bedrooms on the first floor and a restaurant next-door.

Part of the House of Sallust, which was later converted into a boarding house.

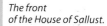

The front of the House of Sallust.

The atrium decorated with 1st style frescoes.

Tomb with altar
of Naevoleya Tyche.

③⑧ THE PORTA ERCOLANO GATE *
AND THE NECROPOLIS

This gate was certainly one of the most important in the town. All the carts and wagons coming from the harbour passed through the Porta Ercolano, as did all commercial traffic heading towards Naples. The gate was also known as the Porta Salis, the Gate of Salt, because it led to the 'Salinae Herculeae' salt works which may have been situated on the coast near the mouth of the river Sarno.

Beyond the Porta Ercolano gate on Via dei Sepolcri we find the tombs built between the founding of the colony (80 B.C.) and the destruction of the town (79 A.D.).

The commonest types of tombs were those with an aedicula, those with an exedra, and those surrounded by a wall or fence with an altar on a podium. However, we also find monumental funeral buildings with seats for the relatives of the dead, such as that of Marcus Cerrinus Restitutus.

Tomb with altar of Caius
Calventius Quietus.

Imaginary reconstruction
of Via dei Sepolcri.

Porta Ercolano.

Tomb with aedicula.

39 THE VILLA OF DIOMEDES

This sumptuous villa was built just outside the Porta Ercolano gate in sight of the town walls.
An entrance on Via dei Sepolcri led straight into the 14-column peristyle around which the various rooms and living quarters of the house were situated. The house's bath area was situated in a triangular space between the road and the peristyle while

The cryptoporticus.

the triclinium/living room opposite commanded a view over the Gulf of Naples and the large garden below. In the centre of the garden was an open-air triclinium with a swimming pool surrounded by a covered gallery (cryptoporticus). Here the master of the house, with his 'treasure' of 1356 sesterces, and 18 other people, mainly heavily bejeweled women, met their death as they tried to flee during the eruption. Their remains were found when the villa was excavated between 1771 and 1774.

View of the summer triclinium and the swimming pool.

Imaginary reconstruction of the garden with a view of the Sorrentine peninsula and the isle of Capri.

The priestess in the sequence of paintings.

40 THE VILLA OF MYSTERIES **

This is the most famous country villa in the whole area around Mount Vesuvius. It can be reached on foot by following the modern road for a short way after leaving the Pompeii archaeological site proper (keep your ticket as this is also valid for entry to the Villa of Mysteries).

The current entrance to the Villa is on the opposite side to the original portal which was situated about 400 metres from the Porta Ercolano gate along the road leading out of the town. The villa owes its fame to the extraordinary wall paintings in the triclinium which make up an almost photographic sequence of theatrical scenes.

The building can be divided into two areas. The main area is exclusively residential and was built in the 2" century B.C. with the sole purpose of providing a luxurious and comfortable place in which to live. The other part is linked to the villa's role as a working farm and hence was built with a view to accommodating the produce of the surrounding countryside. It was added onto the former building in the 1" century A.D.

In the farm area on the right of the main entrance (1), archaeologists found the wine-press that was situated in the rooms where the wine was made (2). On the opposite side of the peristyle (3) are the kitchens, two ovens in the courtyard (4), the lararium and a large lavatory (5).

Beyond the kitchen courtyard we find a bath-house dating from the pre-Roman era which was subsequently used as store rooms (6). These open onto a small four-columned atrium (7) where we also find a number of smaller rooms decorated in the second style, including a cubiculum with two beds (double alcove) (8). The tablinum (9) is embellished with third style decorations on a black background depicting Egyptian figurines and miniaturised elements from the cult of Dionysus.

The tablinum leads into a cubiculum (10) whose original alcoves were made into doorways so as to convert the room into a corridor. The imitation marble decoration is superimposed with panel pictures portraying sacrificial scenes and a fresco of Dionysus with a satyr and dancing maenads. These figures, along with the paintings of sculptures of a dancing satyr, the muse Calliope and Silenus with a hand-servant, set the scene for the nearby 'Triclinium of Mysteries' (11). The latter room, like almost all the residential part of the house, is situated on a three-sided cryptoporticus that had to be built because of the natural slope of the ground and so as to create a colonnade adjoining onto living rooms looking out onto the splendid view of the Gulf of Naples.

Outside view of the villa on the cryptoporticus. In the 1st century A.D. the better-off classes decided to change their way of living. The ancient and noble families now lived permanently in the country villas to get away from the chaos and new lifestyle of Pompeii, characterised by the political and cultural domination of the 'uncultured' traders and businessmen.

Oecus of the villa looking onto the side garden

The Painting of the Mysteries

The cycle of frescoes painted on the walls of the villa's panoramic dining room (11) draws its inspiration from a Greek work of the 4th or 3rd century B.C.. The 'mystery' of the fresco (which is 17 metres long and 3 metres high) lies above all in its interpretation. However, the predominant theory is that the pictures making up the overall composition illustrate the various phases of the initiation of a young woman, perhaps a new bride, to the Dionysiac mysteries.

The orgiastic abandon which typifies the cult of Dionysus is here toned down and occasionally rendered through symbolic references but never with unbridled license.

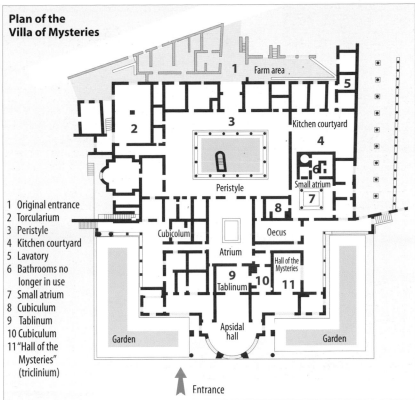

Plan of the Villa of Mysteries

1 Original entrance
2 Torcularium
3 Peristyle
4 Kitchen courtyard
5 Lavatory
6 Bathrooms no longer in use
7 Small atrium
8 Cubiculum
9 Tablinum
10 Cubiculum
11 "Hall of the Mysteries" (triclinium)

Entrance

It must be remembered that the cult of Dionysus was not approved of by the Roman Senate, and harsh penalties were inflicted on initiates in an attempt, often to no avail, to limit or prevent the excesses to which they abandoned themselves during the 'Bacchanalia'.

The huge fresco decorating the so-called "Hall of the Mysteries".

1) The first figure in the sequence.

The sequence of the fresco painting

Starting from the left-hand wall, we can see no less than 28 life-size figures depicted on a podium set against a red background.

The section of the wall in which the door stands depicts a woman wearing a veil, who could be either the matron of the household or a priestess.

The initiate listens to a naked boy (perhaps the youth Dionysus) reading the precepts of the ritual under the watchful eye of the matron or priestess, with one hand on the boy's neck while in the other she holds a rolled parchment.

Next to her we see a young girl carrying a tray of offerings towards a priestess seated between two hand-maidens who are helping her to prepare the sacrifice.

Here the sequence seems to be interrupted by the figure of Silenus leaning on a column and playing the lyre, while a seated satyr (Pan) plays the pipes behind a female panisc suckling a goat at her breast. We are struck by the figure of a woman who is apparently disturbed by the following scenes and seems to be trying to run away, as is suggested by her billowing cape. The sequence continues on the central wall, where we can see Silenus seated and offering a cup to a satyr while another satyr behind him holds up a tragic theatrical mask in an attempt to frighten him by causing its reflection to appear in the wine in the cup. Leaning back on the legs of Ariadne is the god Dionysus, perhaps inebriated or merely exhausted after the frenzy of the orgiastic ceremony. A kneeling woman, the initiate, holds out a hand to remove the veil covering the phallus, the symbol of Dionysus.

Next we see a winged figure flogging a young woman, who is painted on the right-hand wall, kneeling down and looking for protection in the lap of another woman. The naked girl dancing in front of another young woman is a Bacchante seized by the orgiastic frenzy. We then find another bride washing in preparation for her initiation to the mystery. Finally, we see the matron of the household, a priestess of Dionysus, who probably commissioned the 'mystery' to be painted on the walls of her villa.

2) The precepts of the ritual are read out in preparation of the sacrifice.

The room with the fresco painting: photographs 3) and 4).

The wine-press.

The peristyle.

An original painting from the tablinum in the house of Marcus Lucretius Fronto

Itinerary 5

FROM THE PORTA VESUVIO GATE TO THE PORTA DI NOLA GATE

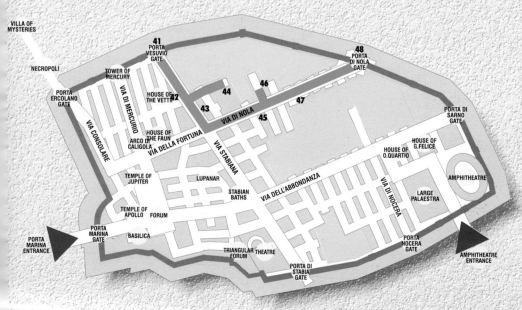

41   PORTA VESUVIO GATE NECROPOLIS

42   * HOUSE OF GILDED CUPIDS

43   HOUSE OF CAECILIUS JUCUNDUS

44   * HOUSE OF SILVER WEDDING

45   HOUSE OF THE CENTENARY

46 ** HOUSE OF M. LUCRETIUS FRONTO

47   HOUSE OF OBELLIUS FIRMUS

48   * PORTA NOLA GATE AND NECROPOLIS

* worth seeing
** not to be missed

The tomb of Vestorius Priscus. This tomb is surrounded by a high wall with a central altar standing on a base containing the burial chamber.
It is entirely decorated with frescoes depicting scenes of hunts and gladiatorial combat and also contains some examples of silverware.
On the south side of the altar base there is a portrait of the deceased in his civic role as an administrator of justice.

41. THE NECROPOLIS AT THE PORTA VESUVIO GATE

Several tombs have been excavated in a necropolis just outside the Porta Vesuvio gate. One worth special mention is the tomb of Caius Vestorius Priscus, one of the town's aediles who died at the age of 22. An inscription indicates that the tomb was built on ground donated by the decurions, who had generously contributed the sum of two thousand sesterces to cover the costs of his funeral.
Near this important gateway to the villas and farms in the countryside to the north of Pompeii we find an example of hydraulic engineering work which was an important part of the town's water supply system. This is the so-called Castellum Aquae, which channelled water from a branch of the Augustan aqueduct from Serino into three pipes to supply the different parts of the town. This feat of engineering was extremely useful and marked a change in the people's habits as, prior to this, they had had to draw water from wells or use rainwater that had been channelled from the house's impluvium into specially built tanks.

View of the archaeological site from the Porta Vesuvio gate.

42. HOUSE OF THE GILDED CUPIDS

Opposite the house of the Vettii, in the triangular-shaped insula on Via Vesuvio, stands the house belonging to the wealthy gens Poppaea - possibly the family of Nero's second wife.
The house obtained its name from the original decoration used for the cubiculum near the shrine of the tutelary gods, where, set into the plaster, there were several glass discs whose gold leaf back bore the engraving of the cupids.
The layout of the house is quite unusual as it has an atrium and tablinum but no cubicula (bed chambers) on either side, and all of this is off-set compared to the rest of the house, which elegantly extends out towards the peristyle and garden.

Rare detail of stucco decorations on a coffered ceiling.

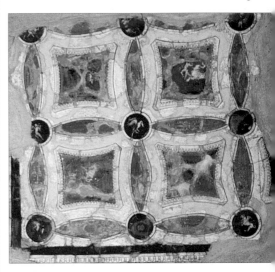

Portrait of a woman found in a cubiculum. Her hairstyle was highly in vogue during the Age of the Emperor Nero.

The latter was lavishly decorated with statuettes, busts, animal sculptures and theatrical masks which were fitted into the walls and hung between the columns, in addition to medallions against the evil eye. Every single object was tastefully designed and added a magical atmosphere to the house. The colonnade along which we find the lararium and, tucked away in one corner, the sacellum dedicated to the Egyptian triad of Harpocrates, Isis and Serapis follows the slope of the ground so that the west-facing side is higher than the rest. Here we find the triclinium with its stone beds and two lavishly decorated rooms: the one on the left, with a vegetable garden to the rear, shows a depiction of the seasons against a white background, while the other (which backs onto the kitchen) is decorated with love-related themes, such as Leda and the swan, Venus fishing, and Actaeon spying on Diana while she bathes. Both rooms have particularly striking coffered ceilings.

The original decoration in the cubiculum where the gilded cupids were found.

The garden of the house.

Bronze portrait of the father of Caecilius Jucundus.

43 THE HOUSE OF CAECILIUS JUCUNDUS

This house, with its classical layout around an atrium and a peristyle, belonged to the banker of Pompeii, and his entire archives consisting of 154 waxed writing tablets dating between 53 and 62 A.D. were found intact. These consisted of sale contracts for land, animals or slaves and receipts for the payment of colonial taxes, as L. C. Jucundus was also the official tax collector. The bronze portrait - commissioned by the freedman Felix - found in the tablinum of the house gives us a clear image of what his father looked like. In this house, researchers found two marble bas-reliefs (both subsequently stolen). One of them depicts the Temple of Jupiter which whose damaged during the earthquake of 62 A.D. and the relevant expiatory sacrifice, while the other depicts the Castellum Aquae with the Porta Vesuvio gate collapsing.

44 HOUSE OF THE SILVER WEDDING   *

This house was named in honour of the Italian royal couple, Umberto and Margherita of Savoy, on the occasion of their silver wedding anniversary in 1893, the same year in which the house was discovered. It is located in the last side street off Via Ve-

suvio, next to an area which has yet to be excavated.

It was built in the 2nd century B.C. and is distinguished by its high atrium with four large Corinthian columns which support the roof, and its bedroom where the sunlight was filtered by means of veils. There are two gardens. The first is in line with the atrium and has its own private bath-house and open-air swimming pool, a large kitchen and garden and an elegant living room. The latter was decorated with a mosaic floor and second style paintings and has four octagonal imitation porphyry columns supporting a barrel-vaulted ceiling. The ceiling of the peristyle is higher on the side which receives most sunlight in order to provide a particularly pleasant area to sit on winter days. The second garden, which is much larger and completely surrounded by a wall, has a pool in the centre and an outdoor triclinium.

Right: cubiculum decorated in the second style.

Bottom right: the impressive tetrastyle atrium in the House of the Silver Wedding

The room with octagonal imitation porphyry columns.

45 HOUSE OF THE CENTENARY

This large house, built in the 2nd century B.C. and restructured during the Imperial age, opens onto Via di Nola and consists of a double Tuscan atrium and a peristyle with a double order of columns at the front. The house was given this name as it was discovered in 1879, the year of the eighteenth centenary of the eruption which completely buried Pompeii. It is divided into two sections: the main house, for the master's family, and the servants' quarters, with a separate entrance from a side street. In line with tradition it has a private bath-house and swimming pool. A particularly beautiful nymphaeum with a fountain is situated at the rear of the peristyle, and a bed chamber in the eastern section of the house is decorated with two highly detailed erotic frescoes. The famous fresco depicting Mount Vesuvius resplendent with woods and vineyards comes from the lararium in the secondary atrium and is now housed in the National Archaeological Museum in Naples.

Painting from the lararium showing Bacchus and Mount Vesuvius resplendent with vineyards.

Dancing maenad.

One of the two erotic paintings which decorated a private bed chamber.

Nymphaeum with fountain.

The medallion depicting a young boy who closely resembles Mercury was found on one side of the door of a bed chamber along with a medallion depicting a baby girl and suggests that the room was used as a children's bedroom.

46 THE HOUSE OF MARCUS ** LUCRETIUS FRONTO

This house is situated in a side street on the Via Nola which has only been partly excavated and which is named after the house. The house itself is well known for refined third style decorations, considered to be superior to those found in Rome. The juxtaposition of shiny black walls with interposed yellow bands depicting arabesques and hunting scenes, and the black floor with inlaid pieces of mar-

ble is particularly unusual. The decorations in the tablinum are worth close examination and depict landscapes with villas and gardens as well as two mythological paintings. The wall to the left illustrates the marriage of Venus and Mars while to the right we can see the Triumph of Bacchus accompanied by Ariadne on a carriage drawn by oxen. In the yellow room to the right of the tablinum, in addition to a group of cupids, a painting with Narcissus looking at his reflection in the water (on the left) and Perona breastfeeding her old father, Myconis (on the right). In the centre of the left wall in the

Landscape with sea-side villas.

Tuscan atrium decorated with third style black paintings. The room in the background is the tablinum.

winter triclinium (immediately after the vestibulum) there is an illustration of a scene taken from Euripides' tragedy 'Andromache', in which Neottoleus is killed by the sword of Orestes on the altar of Apollo. In the next cubiculum there is a 'triumph' of extremely small and intricate details set against a black background, while on the right wall there is a painting of Ariadne bringing Theseus the thread so that he can find his way through the labyrinth. The house extends out towards the back garden, whose walls used to be covered in frescoes depicting hunts for wild beasts and other animals.

The marriage of Mars and Venus.

Narcissus by the fountain.

47 THE HOUSE OF M. OBELLIUS FIRMUS

This house dates back to the Samnite period and was being restored when the volcano erupted. It is built around two atriums and a section of peristyle with a garden. The main atrium is tetrastyle in form, i.e. it has four Corinthian columns supporting the open roof. There is a table on a pedestal (cartibulum) in front of the entrance, between the impluvium and the large tablinum, whereas the lararium is situated in the first right-hand corner. A bronze safe - a clear sign of the family's wealth - is solidly anchored to

the ground near the living room (alae) on the right-hand side of the house. In addition to the fact that it has a tablinum, the importance of the house is also expressed by the size of the adjoining reception hall which opens out onto the peristyle through a wide doorway. A plaster cast of the door is on display. The secondary atrium, which is Tuscan and has no columns, is linked to both the first atrium and the peristyle. The tablinum is situated in this part of the house and is decorated with second style paintings, while the kitchen, which is hidden behind the corridor leading to the peristyle, is annexed to the bathhouse which was heated by the kitchen oven. The house extends towards the garden and the peristyle with its three-sided colonnade, where the reception rooms and sleeping areas are much smaller and still bear some traces of the fine wall decorations.

This was the last house on Via di Nola to be entirely unearthed. One characteristic of this area is that only the rooms of the houses which open out onto the street have been excavated.

Imaginary reconstruction of the atrium in the house.

Porta di Nola gate.

48 THE PORTA DI NOLA GATE AND THE NECROPOLIS

The Porta di Nola gate, built at the end of one of the main town roads, is situated on the edge of the hill of Pompeii. It is a square-shaped gate with two projecting structures, a barrel vault, and an effigy of Minerva on the inside. A necropolis was found at the foot of the town walls outside the gate where excavation work has uncovered several particularly interesting burial monuments. There are three tombs, two of which are semicircular exedrae made of tuff stone from nearby Nuceria with two paws of winged lions poised on the far ends. As can be read on the inscription, one tomb belonged to the wife of a duumvir, Aesquillia Polla, who died at the age of 22. The other tomb is surrounded by a wall, inside which were a cinerary glass urn made and a hole for the libations to the deceased. Marcus Obellius Firmus, who had been elected several times to the position of town administrator, was buried here while his house was situated not far from the Porta di Nola gate. In the same part of the town, in an area presumably the deceased, used for cremating archaeologists have found four graves - identified by the funerary steles - of Pretorian soldiers stationed in Pompeii.

Marble tombstone of M. Obellius Firmus.

Semicircular exedra tomb.

Aerial view of the Via di Nola.

Disegno di Francesco Corni

Itinerary 6

VIA DELL'ABBONDANZA

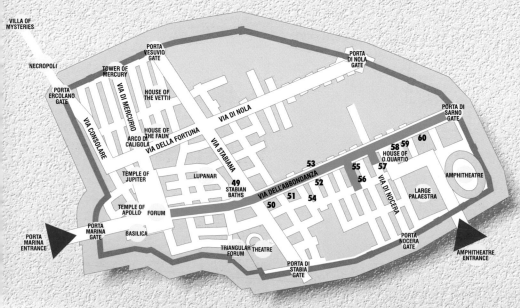

The town's oldest baths complex opens onto Via dell'Abbondanza at the corner of Via Stabiana not far from the Forum and probably dates from the 2nd century B.C.

The establishment covers a total surface area of over 3,500 square metres is divided into two adjacent sections respectively reserved for men and women and includes a courtyard which was used as a gymnasium. Three sides of the courtyard have colonnades (P) with stuccoed tuff-stone pillars, while the fourth side borders onto a large swimming-pool one and a half metres deep (3). Separated from the gymnasium by a low wall, the latter could be reached from two side-rooms (2-4) where the bathers would probably get changed for the bathing rite.

After the earthquake of 62 A.D. the swimming-pool area was embellished with elegant coloured stucco decorations which enclose a number of panels depicting mythological figures and athletes.

Only a few bathing chambers were annexed to the gymnasium to the north. The other rooms were later turned into a large lavatory (6) situated at the rear of the apartment belonging to the manager of the baths.

The bathing establishment proper occupies the longer side of the peristyle. A door in the right-hand corner of the colonnade (7) leads to the men's section. The first room on the left is a chamber for cold

The coloured stuccoes of the barrel vault in the entrance hall of the men's section.

baths (frigidarium) (10), which is round in shape with four corner niches and a pool in the centre. The water used to feed the pool flowed from another niche in the north-facing wall. The fact that this room came before the one where the bathers undressed may suggest that it was actually used as a laconicum, i.e. a steam room in which the air was heated by means of bronze braziers.

From the entrance hall the bather entered the changing room (apodyterium) (9), which is plastered in white except for a red band running all round the lower half of the walls; the vault has stucco decorations in various colours. The next room is the tepidarium (11), in which warm baths were taken. It was heated by hot air which circulated under the floor (between small terra-cotta pillars called suspensurae) and - as can be seen in the areas where work was in progress at the time of the eruption - through cavities in the walls themselves. The room that follows is the calidarium (12) where the tub on the right-hand side was used for hot baths. Above the bath we can see three niches which contained statues while the marble basin situated along the apsidal wall contained cold water which the bathers used to cool off while in that intensely heated room.

The fires for heating both the water and the air needed for the two sections of the bathing complex were situated behind the calidarium wall. Walking along the gymnasium colonnade, we reach the entrance door to the women's section (13). Here the rooms follow one another in the same sequence as in the men's section, but as there is no frigidarium, the bathers would pass directly from the changing room (14) into the tepidarium (15) and from there to the calidarium 16) which contained a number of bronze tubs for individual baths.

The frigidarium.

The gymnasium colonnades.
As the gymnasium is situated in the older core of the 4th century complex, it is generally assumed that the building was originally a palaestra and was changed into a thermal establishment only in the 2nd century B.C.

Seneca's description of the public baths

To get an idea of the public baths as they were around the middle of the 1st century B.C., we can do no better than to refer to an authoritative eye-witness who lived at that time: Seneca. In a letter he dictated the rules that had to be followed if a thermal complex was to satisfy the 'ritual' content of a visit to the baths, and explained that bathers would only enjoy the experience "*if large circular mirrors were placed all round the walls; if Alexandrine marble was embellished with Numidian marble ornamentations; if artistic mosaics in various designs were provided in addition to those marble decorations; if the ceiling was made of glass; if marble from Thasos, which once could only be admired in temples, was used to encircle the tubs in which the bathers used to recover from the extenuating sweating process; and if the water flowed from silver taps*".

The frigidarium. The vault of this room had a skylight and was frescoed in such a way as to create the impression of a star-lit sky; the walls were decorated with garden scenes.

The layout of the Stabian Baths.

Colonnaded Courtyard	
P	Gymnasium
1	Entrance
2	Swimming pool wash basins
3	Swimming pool
4	Swimming pool changing rooms
5	Individual bathing chambers
6	Toilet
Men's Section	
7	Entrance
8	Waiting-room
9	Changing-room
10	Frigidarium
11	Tepidarium
12	Calidarium
Women's Section	
13	Entrances
14	Changing-room
15	Tepidarium
16	Calidarium
17	Laconicum
18	Walking-area

Via dell'Abbondanza

The changing room (apodyterium).

The Statue of Apollo playing the lyre.

The Laundry of Stephanus. Cloth was washed in the impluvium in the atrium.

50 THE HOUSE OF THE LYRE-PLAYER

This large building (approxi 2,700 sq.m) was created by joining two residential complexes which covered an area nearly equal to that of the whole insula. The house can be entered both from Via dell'Abbondanza and from Via Stabiana. It is arranged around two atria and three peristyles, and it is name derives from a bronze statue of Apollo playing the lyre (today in the National Archaeological Museum in Naples). Magnificent paintings and bronze portraits of famous personalities also found in it and are now on shown in the same museum. As is inferred from electoral propaganda and a number of graffiti, it belonged to the Popidius family.

51 THE LAUNDRY OF STEPHANUS ＊

This is the only building in Pompeii which was originally built as a laundry and fuller's workshop; the three other establishments of this kind were restructured residential buildings. The fuller's workshop provided services to numerous clothiers, wool makers and tailors working in the town. According to the electoral slogans painted on the facade ('the united fullers recommend ... Stephanus recommends'), the establishment has been attributed to a certain Stephanus.

A press used to fold cloth was placed against the left wall of the large entrance hall. Past the entrance hall, we enter an atrium with a flat roof which served as a terrace to hang out the washing. Finer

cloth was washed in the large parapeted tank in the middle of the atrium. The peristyle at the rear of the atrium has three intercommunicating stone tubs and, alongside these, five basins where cloth was trodden by foot. A number of vessels containing urine were found nearby. Urine was used to treat the cloth and was collected in terra-cotta amphorae which were stored in separate rooms not far from the workshop itself.

The kitchen and a lavatory are reached through a door in the left-hand corner of the peristyle.

Returning to and crossing Via dell'Abbondanza, we reach the entrance to a shop in which activities linked to those of the laundry were carried out. This is the so-called 'Workshop of Verecundus', which was a felting establishment. As with many buildings in this street, only the facade now remains. The plaster on the facade is covered with illustrated advertisements showing the manufacturing phases of the articles that were made in it, among which felt shoes and ready-made clothes which were sold directly to the public.

A detail of the painted facade of the Workshop of Verecundus.

The Laundry of Stephanus.
A tub for bleaching cloth in urine.

52 THE THERMOPOLIUM (I 8,8) *

Walking further down Via dell'Abbondanza in the direction of the Porta di Sarno Gate, we reach Pompeii's equivalent of a 'fast-food' restaurant, where warm meals could be bought and eaten on the spot. Coins for a total weight of about 3 kg, equivalent in worth to about 680 sesterces, were found in one of the wall recesses. Given the large quantity of change (374 asses and 1,237 quadrantes, each worth one quarter of an as), these were probably the takings of a single day's business. The shop is completed by a sacellum dedicated to Mercury and Dionysus and a small shrine for the tutelary deities of the household. The publican's own apartment extended to the rear of the shop and was reached through an independent entrance door which opened onto a narrow side street. A magnificent specimen of late 3rd-style decoration can be seen in the triclinium.

The 'thermopoliun' on Via dell'Abbondanza is an example of an ancient 'fast-food' restaurant. Warm cooked foods were stored in a masonry counter and were eaten on the spot.

The lararium.

53 ASELLINA'S TAVERN

Behind the facade of the tavern, which borders on Via dell'Abbondanza and is covered all over with election propaganda, we can see a masonry counter which contained four terra-cotta vessels for storing cooked meals.

At the rear of the tavern are the remains of the staircase which led to the guest rooms on the upper floor. The graffiti on the walls of these rooms suggest that customers could also enjoy the company of Asellina's waitresses. The tavern-keeper Asellina as well as Zmyrina, Ismurna and Aegle were influential women who used to sign electoral propaganda to support candidates in the elections for high municipal offices.

The entrance door to Asellina's Tavern and the painted sign still visible on the facade.

54 THE HOUSE OF THE EPHEBE

This residential complex is situated in a side street of Via dell'Abbondanza, not far from the House of Menander, and actually comprises three buildings converted into one. It derives its name from the bronze statue of an Ephebe which was found in the house and was used to support oil-lamps needed to light the triclinium couches during evening receptions. Access to the house was through the second entrance-door and a Tuscan atrium which was flanked to the right by the family's living quarters and, on the left, by the reception rooms and areas devoted to leisure activities and sport. Here, in addition to a few living-rooms, we find a large open triclinium which was once surrounded by a shaded garden with a fountain whose jets were forced through walls decorated with several wild animals and Nile landscapes. Between the atrium and the garden was a small triclinium with plant decorations in the middle of the floor and a still-life with a basket full of fish on the rear wall. A larger triclinium is situated opposite this wall.

Pygmies in a painting situated in the summer triclinium.

The House of the Ephebe. The summer triclinium.

55 THE BAKERY OF SOTERICUS

Some of the excellent bread for which the area around Vesuvius was renowned was made in this bakery on Via dell'Abbondanza opposite the House of Trebius Valens. As the building did not include a shop, the bread produced was evidently sold elsewhere. This was one of the thirty-one bakeries and cake shops in the town and the name of its reputed owner, Sotericus, appears on the front of the inn next-door. The large workshop where bread was made extended across two older buildings and was equipped with shelves, worktops and a dough kneading machine. The workshop also had an oven, a grain warehouse, a bedroom for the workers and four different-size machines driven by donkeys kept in the adjoining stable.

56 THE GARUM WORKSHOP

'Garum' was the name of a fish sauce which was a favourite throughout Pompeii and was prepared and sold in this small house on Via dell'Abbondanza. As the residues found in six sealed containers in the courtyard have not yet been analysed, it has so far been impossible to establish whether the garum produced here was the high quality type (garum excellens or garum flos flos) or some poorer variety. A large number of empty amphorae were stored in the back garden; they had just been cleaned and were ready to be filled by means of a funnel which was also found in the workshop. This is evidence that the garum from Pompeii was exported to many places throughout the Roman Empire. The name of the manufacturer, A. Umbricius Scaurus, was painted on these vessels. Thanks to the commercial success of his product especially in Rome, A. Umbricius Scaurus was able to embark on a political career which culminated in the office of duumvir during the reign of the Emperor Nero.

57 THE HOUSE OF MAGICAL RITES

This is a house where the general public could take part in magical rites.

The name of the complex derives from two 'magic' bronze hands recalling Sabatius, the god of vegetation, that were found in it along with two ritual terra-cotta vases. The latter had embossed decorations in the shape of lizards, snakes, tortoises, grapes and loaves of bread which were probably intended to suggest rural divinities and natural agents. A room not far from the entrance door is supposed to have been used to hold propitiatory meetings and votive banquets. As is suggested by numerous examples of graffiti, the exedra which is reached through a door behind an altar situated in the courtyard was used to perform magical rites.

Above: a charred loaf of bread. On the left: the bakery (The National Archaeological Museum in Naples).

The 'magical' hands are represented in the act of blessing, with ring finger and little finger folded, and the god Sabatius appearing in the palm is surrounded by the symbols of various divinities: the pine-cone of Attis, the caduceus of Mercury and the cymbal and tympanum of Cybele. The woman feeding a baby reproduced on the wrist is evidence that Sabatius was especially worshipped by women during and after their pregnancy.

The amphora warehouse.

VEGETABLES AND GARUM SAUCE

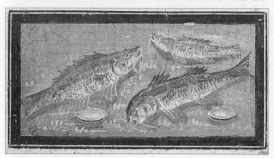

Various everyday lifestyles in Pompeii are documented by finds of household articles and by 'pictures' painted on the walls in numerous rooms. Indeed paintings were used not only for decoration but also as 'catalogues' of family habits and tastes as well as to illustrate the social status of the owner.

Finds of charred foodstuffs informe us of what the Pompeians used to eat. As the Pompeians were essentially traders, their diet was often enriched by delicacies imported from other countries, particularly from north Africa and the Orient.

Basically, Pompeian cuisine was rich in fibre, vegetable proteins and minerals.

Vegetables and fruit were basic components of the Pompeian diet, along with bread, which was made in several bakeries with their own flour mills alongside.

Vegetables were also grown in kitchen gardens and their abundant use in cooking confirms the nickname of 'herb eaters' given to the Romans by Plautus. Pliny the Elder classified about one thousand edible plants, many of which were highly praised for

Examples of these are wicker-baskets full of fresh ricotta cheese, pots filled with the special vegetables grown in kitchen gardens around the town, for instance leek and cauliflower; bowls containing several kinds of fruit such as grapes, figs, chestnuts, apples and pomegranates and compositions depicting poultry and geese, fish and shellfish.

their therapeutic properties.

A famous type of cabbage grown in the area was well known and highly appreciated in Rome under the name of Pompeii cabbage or 'cauliflower'. In 'De Agricultura' Cato praised it as the 'supreme vegetable'.

"If, during a banquet, you intend to drink a lot and eat with appetite - Cato suggests - have some raw cauliflower before and after your meal and you will feel as if you had not eaten anything at all and you can drink as much as you like".

Several kinds of lettuce very similar to those still in use today were grown in the countryside around Pompeii as well as endives, flowering broccoli, basil, carrots, cress and leeks. In addition to onions and garlic, which the poorer classes used not only to season all sorts of dishes but also as their main dish, leeks were classed by Pliny as first-class vegetables.

cherry, apricot and peach trees had become more and more common.

The inhabitants of Pompeii adopted sophisticated procedures to preserve vegetables and fruit. Vegetables for the winter were put in vinegar or brine, while fruit was dried and then preserved in honey, which was also used in large quantities mixed with wine.

Well-known cheeses (caseus) and smoked cheeses, were also made from sheep's or cow's milk.

The Pompeians used to dress their dishes with a sauce, called garum, which was prepared by soaking several kinds of ungutted blue-fish, such as tuna, in brine.

Garum was so popular throughout Pompeii that there were several workshops which produced and sold different blends of this sauce.

This trade was favoured by the existence of the 'Salinae Herculeae' and other large salt-works outside the town walls all along the coast. It was there that brine, the indispensable ingredient of the garum sauce, was produced.

Charred remains of melon seeds, broad beans, peas, chick-peas and lentils provide precise information on what was produced and thus eaten in Pompeii.

Olives were also a favourite in Pompeii; they were grown throughout the countryside toward the Lattari mountains and, as today, were either pickled in vinegar or salt or used to make oil.

Remains of walnuts, chestnuts and almonds have also been found in some houses, where they were stored on shelves as provisions available for family use.

Several kinds of fresh fruit grown throughout the countryside around the town were on sale in the well-stocked town market, including apples, pomegranates, quinces, pears, grapes, figs and plums. In the years immediately before the eruption fruit trees imported from abroad such as

The portrait of Loreius Tiburtinus dressed as a high-priest of Isis.

The paintings in the sacellum dedicated to the goddess Isis.

58 THE HOUSE OF ✳✳
D. OCTAVIUS QUARTIUS

The residential section of this complex is a particularly luxurious building which, although not exceptionally big, boasts the largest garden in Pompeii. The garden has recently been restored and planted with the species of trees which are thought to have originally been grown in it.

The house has a large atrium with numerous bed chambers (cubicula) arranged all round it and its impluvium is surrounded by a low masonry flower bed. The cubiculum which is reached by turning left from the entrance hall contains a stove for baking terra-cotta pots.

A bronze seal found near the stove suggests the house belonged to a certain D. Octavius Quartius, whilst until recently the numerous election slogans painted on its external walls had led archaeologists to assume that it was the property of Loreius Tiburtinus. The room in the bottom left-hand corner was originally a living-room and was later changed into a passage leading to the lavatory and kitchen at the rear of the house. Walking across the atrium we enter a small square peristyle surrounded by a number of rooms, of which the most remarkable is a large reception hall. The lower half of the walls has an imitation marble decoration bordered by two friezes: the lower one portrays the feats of the Greeks at Troy and the upper one illustrates the expedition of Hercules against Laomedon.

One section of the T-shaped water channel in the back garden extends along the width of the building while the second section runs from one end of the garden to the other.

On the right of the first section of the water channel is a room with fourth-style decorations including the image of a high-priest of Isis, suggesting that the room was used as a sacellum for the cult of this goddess. Opposite it, alongside an apsidal fountain, is a biclinium which was used when the family dined in the open air. The frescoes on the bottom walls of the biclinium portray Narcissus at the Fountain (on the right) and Pyramus and Thisbe, the two lovers who committed suicide (on the left).

At the junction of the two water channels is a four-columned aedicula containing a nymphaeum which supplied water to the more than 50-metre-long channel. Originally the garden area was entirely covered with pergolas and enclosed all round by high-trees and was used for the nocturnal rites in honour of the goddess Isis. It is assumed that the two sections of the water channel could be made to flood the whole area in order to imitate the Nile floods to which the fertility of the Egyptian fields was owed.

Narcissus at the fountain.

Pyramus and Thisbe.

An aerial view of the house of Octavius Quartius and the trees all round the garden.
The building on the left is the House of Venus.

A view of the water channel running through the garden of the house.

A WORKING TOWN

Many of the town's inhabitants were farmers, but the town's excellent geographic position with respect to the villages further inland and the location of a river port not far from the sea also gave great impetus to trade.

Several kinds of arts and crafts also played an important role in the local economy. Some workshops were engaged in the whole wool manufacturing process from shearing to tailoring, while the washing and dying process was performed in the fullers' workshops. To bleach cloth the fullers used human urine which was collected directly from Pompeian households where it was stored in 'portable' containers placed alongside the streets. Other workshops produced the famous fish sauce called garum, while bread was made in over thirty bakeries with annexed mills.

Of course there was also a wealth of pottery-makers and ceramists, blacksmiths, joiners and carpenters, marble-carvers, goldsmiths and scriptores, i.e. artisans whose job it was to paint red and black election slogans and other notices to the public, most of which are still visible on the walls.

The wealthiest and most powerful corporation of artisans in the town was that of the wool-makers and clothiers in general, as is confirmed by the imposing building in the Forum which they dedicated to the patron of their trade, the priestess Eumachia.

As the town was a flourishing trading centre, thousands of people would flock towards it every day from the surrounding areas. The hospitia (boarding houses) in which they found accommodation were

Fullers at work. A painting associated with the cloth trade.

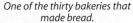

One of the thirty bakeries that made bread.

either annexed to the cauponae (taverns) and thermopolia, where they could have a warm meal as in our modern-day 'fast-food restaurants', or to the tabernae, which served the excellent wine from the vineyards on the slopes of Mount Vesuvius. Numerous, mostly one-room shops ran all along the main streets and all kinds of articles were on sale on masonry counters.

Almost every family - even the relatively wealthy ones - used to rent out rooms to passing tradesmen since it was an easy source of income. In many cases the owners were also directly in charge of sales, as is witnessed by the passageways between the residential areas of the houses and the shops.

Hordes of pedlars would travel to Pompeii every day to sell their goods on strategically placed stalls throughout the town, for example in the Forum and the surroundings of the Amphitheatre and especially near the town gates and along the banks of the river in the harbour.

A painted advertisement: a felter's shop.

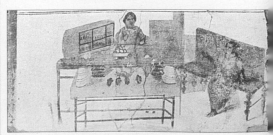

59 THE HOUSE OF VENUS ✳

The focal point of this house is the peristyle, which is sumptuously decorated with painted garden features (fountains, hedges, birds, flowers, sculptures). The most impressive painting of all is on the rear wall: it portrays a naked Venus with a head of curly hair and resplendent with gold jewels, sailing in a shell with billowing sails accompanied by a retinue of cupids. From an artistic point of view the painting is of poor quality, but its colours are well arranged and the overall effect is highly dramatic.

Panel with a view of the sea.

The large fresco of 'Venus in the shell'.

The peristyle and the garden.

A detail of one of the rectangular marble columns with its Corinthian capital.

An aerial view.

60 THE HOUSE OF JULIA FELIX*

Thanks to its large size and particular typology, this house can be defined a 'villa'. It extends over an area corresponding to two insulae, of which one-third is occupied by the building proper and two-thirds were used as a vegetable garden.

After the earthquake of 62 A.D., the owner of this sumptuous and elegant house, Julia Felix, daughter of Spurius, decided to ease the difficulties caused by the shortage of accommodation by renting out part of the house. As the Forum Baths could be used only in part, she also opened her private baths to the public. The notice painted on the facade reads 'elegant bathing facilities, shops with annexed apartments upstairs and independent apartments on the first floor are offered for rent to respectable people'. Also the maximum lease term, a period of five years 'from August 1st next to August 1st of the sixth year', is specified.

The house was divided into three parts. The baths, with access from Via dell'Abbondanza, were provided with all the required facilities and an open swimming-pool. The owner's apartment looks out onto a magnificent garden with a water channel surrounded on all sides by original marble-embellished quadrangular columns. Lastly there were the shops, some of which opened onto Via dell'Abbondanza and some onto the side-street leading to the Large Palaestra. The rented lodgings were also situated on this side-street.

The sculptures which decorated the garden and some of the paintings found in the house are now on show at the National Archaeological Museum in Naples, while a fresco with Apollo and the Muses is exhibited in the Louvre, Paris.

The original colonnades of the House of Julia Felix, which was first unearthed in 1755.

An aerial view of the Amphitheatre and the Large Palaestra.

Itinerary 7

FROM THE PORTA NOCERA GATE TO THE AMPHITHEATRE

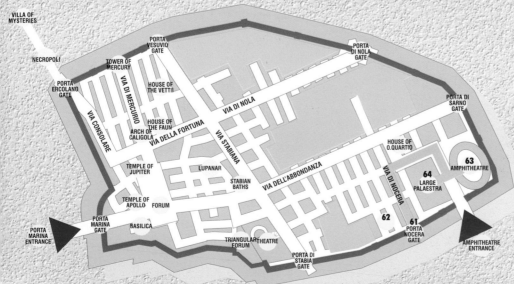

61   NECROPOLIS AT THE PORTA NOCERA
62 * GARDEN OF THE FUGITIVES
63 ** AMPHITHEATRE
64   LARGE PALAESTRA

* worth seeing
** not to be missed

The funeral pillar of Titus Suedius Clemens a prefect sent to the town by the Emperor Vespasian to discourage the unauthorized use of land.

61 THE NECROPOLIS OUTSIDE * THE PORTA NOCERA GATE

A wealth of tombs which formed the town's necropolis have been unearthed along a 250-metre stretch of the road running along the town walls just outside the Porta Nocera gate.

A monumental exedra-shaped tomb is dedicated to Eumachia, the priestess of the cult of Venus to whom a building in the Forum is dedicated.

Further on is the Tomb of the Flavius family: eight of its niches are situated over the door and some of the six niches on either side are decorated with tuff-stone busts and inscriptions. Some of the most interesting of these are high-podium tombs such as the one of Publius Vesonius Phileros or the four-niched tomb of Marcus Octavius, one of the veterans that settled in the town after it had been conquered by Silla. The former is of particular interest because of a long inscription in the middle of the podium. Complaining of having been unjustly accused by a friend, Vesonius addresses passers-by with the words: *"If it is not too much of an inconvenience, stop here for a moment and learn about the dangers you should be wary of. The man whose name is mentioned below and who - so I thought - was my friend brought false charges against me. Through the intervention of the gods and thanks to my innocence I was acquitted of every charge in court. My hope is that the person who has slandered me will be rejected by the gods of the household and those of the after-world"*.

The Porta Nocera gate and a stretch of the town-wall.

The tomb of the Octavius family.

The tomb of the Flavius family.

The necropolis outside the Porta Nocera gate.

62 THE GARDEN OF THE FUGITIVES ✳

The name given to this rural dwelling reflects the dramatic events that took place in its large vegetable garden.

The house is situated in the area around the Large Palaestra in the vicinity of the Porta Nocera gate. More than any other, the scene which unfolds in the Garden of the Fugitives revives the full horror of the tragic death suffered by the inhabitants of Pompeii during the eruption of Vesuvius in 79 A.D.

We can see the plaster casts of the bodies of thirteen people, among them whole families of young people with their children, who met their death while trying to save their lives by fleeing towards the town gates in the direction of the sea.

The Garden of the Fugitives. This group of victims of the eruption was discovered in 1961.

The bodies of eleven other victims, including a pregnant woman, have recently been found not far from the Garden of the Fugitives.

The entrance gallery to the Amphitheatre.

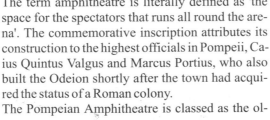

63 THE AMPHITHEATRE **

The term amphitheatre is literally defined as 'the space for the spectators that runs all round the arena'. The commemorative inscription attributes its construction to the highest officials in Pompeii, Caius Quintus Valgus and Marcus Portius, who also built the Odeion shortly after the town had acquired the status of a Roman colony.

The Pompeian Amphitheatre is classed as the oldest of all existing buildings of this kind.

To allow easy access, it was built in an area on the outskirts of the town with comparatively few buildings and it was inserted into a corner formed by the town walls in order to make use of the existing embankments on two of its sides.

About 20,000 people could be seated in its three tiers and would attend bloody shows performed by gladiators and wild animals.

No shows were held in the amphitheatre in the winter months and in the warmest period of the year. In summer, a canopy of dark flax material was fitted above the seats to protect the audience from the burning sun and this was advertised in the notices announcing the shows. The canopy was supported on wooden poles inserted into stone rings fixed to the walls on the upper landings of the stairways.

A number of external stairways led to the upper tiers (summa cavea) which formed the top part of the structure. From a passageway running parallel to the perimeter of the arena, and from here over several stairways, the spectators could reach the middle and lower tiers (ima cavea and media cavea). Carts would enter the amphitheatre through two corridors which led to the slightly flattened ends of the arena directly from outside.

The wild animals used for the shows entered the arena through a narrow passage in the middle of the arena.

The arena of the Amphitheatre.

For reasons still unknown, during the gladiatorial games in 59 A.D. a violent brawl broke out between spectators from Pompeii and others from the nearby town of Nuceria and many people were killed or wounded. As is reported by Tacitus, the people from Nuceria came off worse and this unprecedented incident was discussed in the Roman Senate at the request of Nero. The Pompeian Amphitheatre was closed for ten years and all the 'fan clubs' and supporters' organizations were disbanded and outlawed. Through the intercession of Nero's second wife Poppaea the period of disqualification was subsequently shortened and the Amphitheatre resumed its activity after 62 A.D..

Gladiatorial games.

64 THE LARGE PALAESTRA

This was the largest of all the public spaces reserved for the use of young people. During the age of Augustus the Palaestra was a gymnasium and the sports activities performed in it were intended to serve as a means of propaganda to inculcate the Imperial ideology in the minds of the younger generations. In compliance with a decree issued by the Emperor, the town's youths were organized into associations called 'collegia iuvenum'. The palaestra measures 141 metres by 107 metres and is surrounded by a high wall with ten entrance gates. On three sides it is enclosed by colonnades of 48 columns on the longer side and 35 columns on each of the shorter sides.

A double row of plane-trees (the plaster casts of whose roots can be seen here) grew all along its sides to provide shade for the sports ground.

The gymnasium was completed by a swimming-pool measuring 35 metres by 22 metres and situated right in the middle of the palaestra.

Herculaneum. House of the Stags.

BEYOND POMPEII

HERCULANEUM
OPLONTIS
STABIAE
BOSCOREALE
THE MODERN TOWN OF POMPEI

Oplontis. The Villa of Poppea.

HERCULANEUM
THE ARISTOCRACY'S HOLIDAY RESORT

Archaeologists are now certain that Herculaneum was a predominantly residential town with a high standard of living, inhabited and visited by well-off and refined people, and was also a much sought after holiday resort.

The Patrician class in Rome would leave the capital almost en masse to spend long holidays here and, as a result, the fields around the town were a veritable constellation of luxurious aristocratic villas within a stone's throw of Naples and Pompeii. The town's residential vocation was revived in the 18th century when many sumptuous baroque 'Vesuvian Villas' were built along the 'Golden Mile', the road leading up to the royal residence of Charles III of Bourbon at Portici.

The archaeological confirmation of the town's 'status' was provided by recent discoveries in two areas overlooking the ancient harbour of Herculaneum. Just a short way downhill from the Suburban Baths, archaeologists found a huge pile of skeletons with numerous gold bracelets, rings set with precious engraved stones, gold and silver coins in cloth purses, in addition to numerous gold neckla-

Fountain of Hercules

House of the Stags. Garden with Triclinium.

A pair of gold bracelets and a pile of coins.

ces, chains and ear rings which have all emerged as new from the thick blanket which had engulfed them.

Recent excavations have brought to light other relics previously unfound in the area. For example, a wooden box, still intact and containing a surgeon's instruments, which allows us to see the forefather of the modern scalpel, and an exquisitely made onyx container which has been defined as the 'pro-

'totype' of the modern coffee cup. The 'residential' Herculaneum - wealthy, luxurious and refined - is counterposed to the trading town of Pompeii nouveau-riche, uncultured and noisy, inhabited by astute businessmen and traders who tried in vain to imitate the in-bred refinement of their neighbours in Herculaneum.

The streets and houses of Herculaneum were an evident expression of the affluence of the townspeople and the sense of taste which they had acquired by mingling with scholars who had studied Greek culture.

Many houses are veritable jewels of architecture, rich in beautiful wall decorations and superb floors with mosaics or coloured marble motifs. Many examples of carved wooden ornaments and furnishings have been found almost intact in Herculaneum due to the fact that the eruption of Mount Vesu-

Satyr with wineskin from the House of the Stags.

Mosaic fountain from the House of Neptune and Amphitrite.

Tavern with amphorae on the fourth north-south road.

vius in 79 A.D. caused the town to be covered first by a thick blanket of mud that protected much of the town and its contents from the more devastating effects of the eruption.

Thus we find a number of pieces of wooden furniture: cabinets with opening doors, chests and box-seats and small shrines dedicated to the household gods. One particularly fine piece was found in the

Mercury from the triclinium of the House of the Stags.

Entrance to the Samnite House.

House of the Mosaic Atrium. The floor was deformed under the weight of the solidified mud.

House of the Beautiful Courtyard: a small table with three legs decorated with carved children's heads encrusted with ivory or semi-precious stones in the eye-sockets.

In the House of the Wooden Wall we find a well-preserved mobile partition wall that divided the atrium from the tablinum overlooking a sumptuous garden.

The houses and gardens in Herculaneum were often adorned with precious bronze sculptures and decorations embellished with gold and silver, such as the statue of the youthful Dionysus, and some parts of furniture, for example a horse's head in inlaid silver which was part of the backrest of a couch in the main dining room.

Other fine works include the mosaic of small glass paste tiles decorating the nymphaeum in the summer dining room of the House of Neptune and Amphitrite, and the scenographic atrium in the Samnite House. Even some of the less sumptuous houses were built using original construction features: the House of the Wooden Frame even had a balcony.

However, the true symbol of the economic and cultural wealth of Herculaneum lies outside the walls of the ancient Roman town.

Here stood a majestic villa whose sea-facing side measured more than 250 metres and which many have attributed to Lucius Calpurnius Piso Caesonius, Caesar's father-in-law. Nowadays it is known as the Villa of the Papyrus Scrolls.

When the Bourbons explored this huge residence in 1750, they discovered a fine collection of exquisite bronze sculptures and an important library of Greek texts copied onto several thousand papyrus scrolls.

Many of these and the sculptures found in the villa are now exhibited in the National Archaeological Museum in Naples. This was undoubtedly a place where aristocrats and intellectuals would meet to listen to Epicurean texts, whose readings would help them to find relief from the toils of politics and better appreciate the pleasures of life. Here they could take in the beauty of nature, eat fine food and enjoy 'la dolce vita'.

A Maenad.

House of the Tuscan Colonnade. Small painting of a Maenad with a satyr.

College of the Augustales. Deification of Heracles.

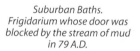

Suburban Baths. Frigidarium whose door was blocked by the stream of mud in 79 A.D.

Seated on comfortable couches in the villa's peristyles, they could contemplate the view of the Gulf of Naples and listen to the singing of the many birds that made their homes in the beautiful countryside around Mount Vesuvius.

This villa lay beneath 27 metres of compressed mud and rock-hard lava, but now a project to excavate the site under the auspices of the Pompeii Archaeological Office is under way.

In the near future archaeologists aim to bring to light what was held to be one of the most beautiful and opulent villas of the Roman world and hopefully find another part of the library housing the Latin manuscripts.

THE SEDUCTRESS POPPAEA IN THE VILLA OF OPLONTIS

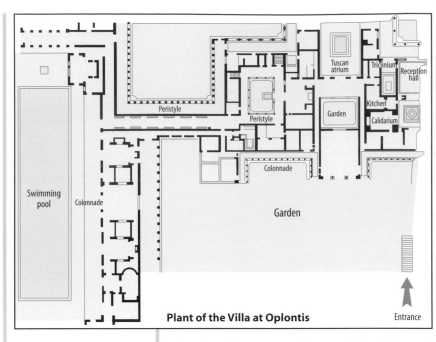

Plant of the Villa at Oplontis

Swimming pool
Colonnade
Peristyle
Peristyle
Tuscan atrium
Triclinium
Reception hall
Garden
Kitchen
Calidarium
Colonnade
Garden
Entrance

If you want to discover the secrets of the high standard of living of the Roman patricians and the pleasurable existence they led both on the green slopes of Mount Vesuvius and in the crystal blue waters of the Gulf of Naples, you can do no better than to dive into the past captured forever in the villa of the 'divine Poppaea', wife of the Emperor Nero. In addition to the villa of Poppaea at Oplontis archaeologists have also unearthed the villa of L. Crassius Tertius, where they found numerous pieces of gold jewelry known as the 'Gold of Oplontis'.

Visitors to the Villa of Poppaea, who was a member of the Pompeian family of the gens Poppaea, can walk over the grounds that once belonged to the 'first lady' of the Roman empire. Seductive and

The second style frescoes in the Villa of Poppaea are held to be the best of their kind, not only from the area around Mount Vesuvius but, indeed, from the whole Roman Empire.

scheming, Poppaea used her considerable sexual charm to achieve her political ends and was the 'puppeteer' pulling the strings of many eminent citizens in Rome.

This majestic residence overlooking the sea was the meeting place of imperial Rome's 'high so-

ciety'. Here they whiled away their time swimming in the sea, relaxing in the huge swimming pool and bathing in ass's milk and dedicated their full attention to the lady of the household.

This villa has more than one hundred rooms laid out in a grandiose and refined architectural style, most of which were embellished by colourful and exquisitely executed frescoes. The residence was divided into three large areas. Two of these were symmetrical and were laid out along a central axis comprising the atrium, the entrance hall, a small garden and a large living room opening out onto the majestic garden facing Mount Vesuvius. The first area had a facade measuring more than 100 metres overlooking the sea and was the residential part of the house, while the other was laid out around a colonnade and was used as the servants' quarters. The third area was an extension to the villa and was centred around the huge swimming pool measuring 60 metres by 18 metres. Rooms were laid out along three sides of the pool while the remaining long side was planted with tall trees.

However, the frescoes on the walls of the villa are the main source of wonder for the visitor. At Oplontis we can finally grasp the true importance of wall-paintings in the rooms where they were to be viewed. Here we can see the revolution in painting that took place with the introduction of the Pompeian second style, which added a new cultural element to residential life.

The concept of a home that was closed and centred merely on itself, and therefore also reflected in the decorations imitating marble slabs, is abandoned in favour of a desire to open up the dwelling to the

This marble group shows a Satyr and Hermaphrodite sculpted in the attempt to have sexual intercourse. It was situated on one of the shorter sides of the swimming pool.

outside world. The depiction of gardens with colonnades allows the interior to be juxtaposed and integrated with the open spaces and colours of nature.

The house thus 'opens out', not physically but thro-

Numerous architectural features in the wall paintings are enhanced by objects depicted with sheer mastery. Over two wicker baskets, one full of figs and the other containing fruit, a transparent veil has been placed in a superbly executed illusion of colour. Other examples include a glass jar of pomegranates, a bow and a quiver of arrows, a theatrical mask, a number of birds including numerous peacocks depicted in a variety of positions and sizes, the most beautiful of which is undoubtedly the one in the living room of Apollo.

ugh the illusion created by pictorial compositions. The architectural element and its view in perspective break down the monolithic walls and lead the eye towards new and fantastic landscapes. The extraordinary features of this villa are further enhanced by its relation with the viridarium (gardens) and the water in the sea below, in the swimming pool and in the fountains, as the garden ran round three sides of the house while the fourth looked directly out to sea. The villa also had rooms in the garden itself (along the swimming pool) which were superbly decorated with frescoes depicting fantastic natural architectures created by the portrayal of plants, fountains and birds in flight. Water sprung forth from sculptures to supply ponds and tanks in which the fountain provided natural music for the garden.

The south-facing side of the villa had an uninterrupted view out to sea with living rooms, exedrae and terraces where guests could take in the beautiful panorama of the Sorrentine peninsular and the isle of Capri.

This majestic sense of space is heightened in the area around the swimming pool, which is further embellished on two sides with a sequence of marble statues, including a highly realistic group por-

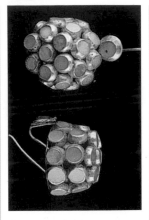

A pair of gold ear-rings found in the Villa along with other jewellery.

Oplontis was a suburb of Pompeii with its country houses and farms laid out along the coast and around the baths complex.

traying a satyr and a hermaphrodite captured in an attempt to have sexual intercourse. Other fine sculptures include a pair of centaurs and another, extremely rare pair of female centaurs, a winged victory copied from an original Greek work, and a neo-Attic crater modified into a fountain around which we can see a group of dancing warriors in a composition known as the 'Pyrrhic Dance'. There is no limit to the fine details that visitors can enjoy by simply letting their imagination be guided by Poppaea, the persuasive matron of the household who will heartily welcome all visitors to her villa at Oplontis.

THE VILLAS OF STABIAE HAVE THE MOST BEAUTIFUL PAINTINGS

A leading artist of the Roman school of fresco painting must certainly have worked in the town of Stabiae. The beauty of the wall paintings in the sumptuous villas unearthed at Castellammare di Stabia - a town on the coastline below Mount Vesuvius, just a short way from Pompeii and at the gateway to the Sorrentine peninsular - is unequalled either in Pompeii or Herculaneum.

Experts have even gone so far as to say that the discovery of the frescoes at Stabiae will require a whole chapter of the history of classical art to be rewritten.

The remains of this Roman settlement, on whose shores Pliny the Elder died, currently include a few country houses the most important of which are the Villa of Ariadne and the Villa of San Marco. These are situated on the Varano hillside looking down onto the Gulf of Naples and the nearby town of Pompeii on the slopes of Mount Vesuvius. However, not a single trace remains of the town itself: in 89 B.C. during the Social War, Silla ordered the total destruction of the 'strategic town of Stabiae' for having taken part in the revolt of the Italic peoples

The Antiquarium at Stabiae. Fragments of wall paintings: a mask of Jupiter Ammonis and, on the right, a cupid playing a timbrel.

A room in the baths area (Villa at S. Marco).

against Rome. What later led the ancient Romans to build luxury villas and farmhouses in the area was the healthy climate, the fertile soil and the wealth of mineral water springs which still make Castellammare di Stabia a famous spa town today.

The first explorations carried out by the Bourbon archaeologists between 1749 and 1782 discovered 6 residential villas and 10 farmhouses. Then, after numerous findings had been carried off together with parts of frescoes, the tunnels that had been used during the explorations were filled in again and Stabiae was completely forgotten for nearly two centuries.

We owe its rediscovery to Libero D'Orsi, the headmaster of a school in Castellammare di Stabia, whose goal in life was to excavate Stabiae which, like Pompeii, Herculaneum and Oplontis, had been buried by the eruption of Mount Vesuvius in 79 A.D.. On the morning of 9 January 1950, accompanied by a school caretaker and an unemployed youth, D'Orsi set off on the adventure he had so often dreamed of. This wistful man was so full of enthusiasm that he managed to convince both the then archaeological superintendent Amedeo Maiuri, who was extremely busy with men and machines excavating the site of Pompeii, and the town council of Castellammare di Stabia which financed the initial research. The results of this work were not long in coming and the archaeologist-headmaster's enthusiasm snowballed. International cultural organisations were now taking an interest in Stabiae. Four villas were unearthed and an antiquarium was set

Villa of S. Marco. A niche between two semi-columns near the swimming pool. Its stuccoed decorations depicted Neptune, Venus and a number of athletes.

The colonnade and swimming pool in the garden of the Villa of S. Marco.

up in the cellars of his school. The museum now houses numerous original relics which point to the culture and artistic refinement of the town of Stabiae and can be found in the town centre near the Via Nocera station of the Circumvesuviana railway.

The most impressive building is undoubtedly the Villa of San Marco.

This complex, which dates from the Augustan age and has a large and sophisticated baths area, was extended in the mid 1" century A.D. The additions to the original rooms set out around an atrium include a large garden with a colonnade, an open gallery above the house and a long narrow swimming pool which ended in an apse whose wall was embellished with a series of niches decorated with exquisite coloured stucco bas-reliefs.

The swimming pool was essentially an ornamental feature although it may sometimes have been used for water games to entertain guests staying there. Laid out the pool were a number of symmetrically alongside rooms decorated with frescoes that are particularly rich in fascinating details.

And it was these wall paintings and also the particularly fine frescoes on the ceilings of the Roman villas at Stabiae that were the most original and innovative feature of painting traditions in the Pompeii area. Here, the canons of fresco painting were 'revolutionised': the bold outline of the figures, the

*Villa of Ariadne.
A cubiculum decorated in
second style: painted Ionic
columns and panels
imitating marble slabs.*

clearly defined chiaroscuro and the linear composition of the figures were abandoned in favour of bold brush strokes and sharp contrasts in light to give life to the works and endow them with the ability to transmit the subject matter and the emotions of the fresco.

"A franker and freer manner", wrote Amedeo Maiuri in 1956, "departing from the academic and classical style to which formal Pompeian painting on the whole remains tied, and yet at the same time a bolder use of colour and a richer modulation of expression in the faces and hands suggests that the artists in this part of Italy better than elsewhere succeeded in adding the warmth of their natural temperament to the Hellenistic tradition from which painting in Campania undeniably descends".

*The tiles decorating the walls of a room
in the Villa of Ariadne.*

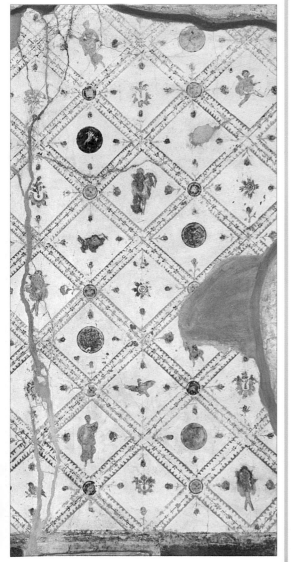

THE BOSCOREALE ANTIQUARIUM

A MUSEUM DOCUMENTING THE EVERYDAY LIFE OF THE PEOPLE OF ANCIENT POMPEII

Archaeology is usually identified with the search for past relics that have a purely artistic value, as monuments and works of art more than anything else stimulate the imagination and instill a sense of admiration. However, this tends to create a view of our ancestors as people who spent their lives in an environment of luxury and works of art. And archaeological museums often seem to consolidate this widespread, though mistaken, belief by focussing on the most beautiful exhibits while virtually neglecting the everyday objects and the role they played in the daily life of the people. Nevertheless, such objects are undoubtedly the ones that characterise a people or community and mark it out from another.

The Boscoreale Antiquarium fills this gap as it is the first museum to be dedicated to the history of the natural environment in the Roman age. Man and his environment in the area around Mount Vesuvius is thus the designated subject of the youngest and most original archaeological museum in Italy.

The Museum is situated in an outlying area of the town of Boscoreale, just over two kilometres from the Porta Marina entrance to the archaeological site of Pompeii, and can be reached by car.

Here, for the first time, archaeology interacts with botany, paleontology and agronomy. Data has been analysed in order to identify the condition of the environment, the plants, the animals, agricultural and

Villa Regina.
The outlines of a ship scratched on a pillar in the portico.

farming techniques and, more generally, the lifestyles of the peoples living around Mount Vesuvius and their relationship with the surrounding environment.

The eruption of 79 A.D. effectively 'sealed' all this information beneath the lava: information which gives us a unique view of ancient history, a sort of 'snapshot' which archaeologists have been examining for 250 years.

On the basis of exhibits of natural objects and archaeological finds, the museum follows an itinerary that starts from an imaginary landing on the coastline below Mount Vesuvius; it then heads inland across the lowland plains and marshes along the river Sarno, through the flourishing vineyards on the foothills of Vesuvius up to the woodland with its rich wildlife which extends almost to the summit of the volcano.

There is also a section of the museum dedicated to the town of Pompeii. The ornamental and vegeta-

Imaginary reconstruction of the countryside just outside Villa Regina.
The vegetation has been reproduced based on the findings of palaeobotanical researches and the results of the excavation work.

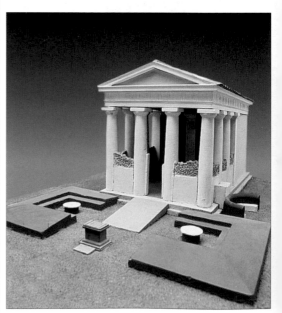

ble gardens of the houses and villas are described through objects, tools and photographs of wall decorations. Visitors are explained the domestic and economic role of the gardens planted with vegetables, fruit, medicinal herbs and even plants used for celebratory purposes. The latter were used in the making of crowns and wreaths to decorate altars and tombs, as can be seen in the House of the Vettii in Pompeii where a painting depicts cupids busily preparing floral crowns.

One particularly significant exhibit is a charred bunch of 88 species of spontaneous herbs that were used as forage for the animals. There are also charred remains of walnuts, figs, almonds and cereals, such as millet, wheat, oats, barley and emmer.

The museum also houses the cooking utensils, mill stones, earthenware jars, sickles, pick-axes and furniture discovered in a number of farms unearthed around Boscoreale over the last 100 years. At the turn of the 19th century, the owners of the surrounding farmlands paid out of their own pockets to unearth the Villa of Publius Fannius Sinistor (where splendid wall paintings now exhibited at the National Archaeological Museum in Naples and at the Metropolitan Museum in New York were found), as well as the Villa of Pisanella with its superb collection of embossed silver tableware (now exhibited at the Louvre in Paris).

Right alongside the museum itself, recent excavations have brought to light a farm that specialised

Antiquarium. White marble statuette representing a female tutelary deity. On the right: charred seeds.

Villa Regina and, in the background, the Antiquarium at Boscoreale.

in wine-making. Here we can admire the remains of the wine-press and the large wine-cellar with its huge earthenware jars, buried in the ground up to their necks. This was where the wine-makers stored the fine wine known as vinum vesuvinum, which the Romans would sometimes drink mixed with honey. A botanic garden has been set up outside the villa and antiquarium to show visitors the

Above: wine-cellar with 18 large earthenware jars (capacity 10,000 litres) buried in the ground up to their necks. Below: the colonnade.

plants and shrubs that made up the flora that either grew spontaneously or was cultivated in the 1st century A.D.. These include fruit trees, such as hazelnuts, peaches and apricots, which were usually planted in the gardens of the houses, and plants used in medicine, textile manufacturing, dyeing and carpentry, in addition to sacred plants.

The museum's display cabinets also house specimens that explain the relationship between the ancient Romans and the sea, their source of fish and seafood. One exhibit shows an amphora with the charred remains of 'garum', the famous hot sauce obtained by fermenting various varieties of bluefish; elsewhere we can examine fishing nets and hooks and even shells, including cowrie shells which were considered powerful amulets against sterility and venerial disease. There is also an extremely rare exhibit of a mollusc called anodonta cygnea, which is now extinct but which the People of Pompeii ate avidly after taking them from the once clear waters of the river Sarno.

Given that the lifestyle in the modern age is characterised by a 'return to nature', a visit to the Boscoreale Antiquarium is a 'must' if we are to draw on the experience of the ancient Romans.

THE MODERN TOWN OF POMPEII

Following the eruption of 79 A.D. every trace of the ancient town of Pompeii was lost. Only a vague memory of the town was preserved in the name Civita (town) which was given to the countryside that now covered the ancient town. No dwellings were built in the area, which was generically referred to as the 'Vallum' or 'Valley' and was characterised by an unhealthy climate due to swamps and marshes. The modern town of Pompei, which was originally called 'Valle di Pompeii' (Valley of Pompeii) was founded in 1875 with a small settlement of 300 people. Today Pompei has a population of about 25,000 inhabitants. The history of the modern town is entwined with the work of an extraordinary man called Bartolo Longo, a devoutly religious layman who spent his whole life spreading the cult of

View of the Sanctuary and the bell-tower.

the Virgin Mary. A lawyer by profession, Bartolo Longo came to the rural district that was to become the town of Pompeii in 1872 as he had been empowered to manage the estate of the Countess De Fusco. Faithfully following his inspiration and with the support of the then Bishop of Nola, he started building a church dedicated to Our Lady of the Rosary.

The miraculous works achieved by the intercession of the Virgin Mary drew people from near and far while generous financial offerings made it possible to start construction work on the Sanctuary, which is now a place of pilgrimage.

In 1887 Bartolo Longo dedicated his full attention to the problems of young orphan girls and later, in 1892, to the sons of convicts and finally, in 1922, to their daughters, setting up homes and schools for them. Bartolo Longo died on 5 October 1926 and was laid to rest in the Chapel that was dedicated to him in 1983. On 7 May 1934 a canonical procedure was initiated for his beatification, which culminated in Rome on 26 October 1980, when Pope John

Paul II defined him as "the layman who lived his religious commitment to the full". The monument built in 1962 on the eastern side of the large square that bears Blessed Bartolo Longo's name is dedicated to this devout man. The bell tower alongside the basilica was built in 1925 and is crowned with a large bronze cross which can be seen from everywhere in the Sarno river valley and serves almost as a lighthouse for all those heading towards Pompei.

The original church was extended in 1939 to create the modern sanctuary that we can see today. The main facade was inaugurated on 5 May 1901 after eight years' work under the supervision of the architect Giovanni Rispoli. Bartolo Longo intended the church to be a monument to Universal Peace built with the small offerings of people from all over the world.

The inside of the sanctuary is embellished with marble decorations, mosaics and paintings but the central feature is the Image of Our Lady of the Rosary which thousands of pilgrims come to visit every year. The painting was restored first in 1875 and subsequently in 1879 before a definitive work of restoration and preservation was carried out in 1965 by the Olivetian Benedictine order in Rome.

The image of the Virgin Mary was crowned by Pope Paul VI and then transported to Pompeii in

The statue of the Virgin on top of the facade of the Sanctuary.

A view of the B. Longo square from the bell tower.

The Sanctuary and its bell tower by night.

triumph by its faithful followers.

The thousands of ex-voto offerings donated to the Virgin Mary in recognition of the protection received from the Madonna are exhibited in one wing of the Sanctuary. Here visitors can admire the decorations, precious chalices, corals and cameos, silver statues and numerous paintings describing the various miracles worked. The large square in the centre of Pompei was inaugurated in 1887 together with the Via Sacra. Pompei officially became a town in its own right on 17 December 1927. The town's economy is predominantly based on tourism and relies a number of hotels, restaurants and elegant shops where visitors can while away their time.

Inside the Basilica.

The painting with the Holy Virgin above the central altar in the Sanctuary.

The Mount Vesuvius Museum

This small natural history museum is dedicated to its founder Gian Battista Alfano and houses an interesting collection of rare minerals gathered during the past eruptions of Mount Vesuvius. A particularly interesting part of the museum exhibits prints, etchings and photographs of the volcano. The museum is currently housed in the premises belonging to the Works of the Sanctuary and is run by the local Tourist Board. Entry is free of charge.

SANCTUARY OPENING HOURS

October-April
Weekdays:
7 a.m. - 2 p.m.; 3 - 7 p.m.
Sundays and Holidays:
6 a.m. - 2 p.m.; 3 - 8 p.m.

May-September
Weekdays:
7 a.m. - 2 p.m.; 3 - 7.30 p.m.
Sundays and Holidays:
6 a.m. - 2 p.m.; 3 - 9 p.m.

Masses
6 a.m. (Sund.s and holid.s)
- 7 - 8 - 9 - 10 - 11 - 12 a.m.
- 1 p.m. (Sund.s and holid.s)
4 - 5 - 6.30 - 7 (weekd.s
May-Sept.) - 7.30 - 8.30
(holids. May-Sept.) p.m.
Rosary said every day
at 6.00 p.m.

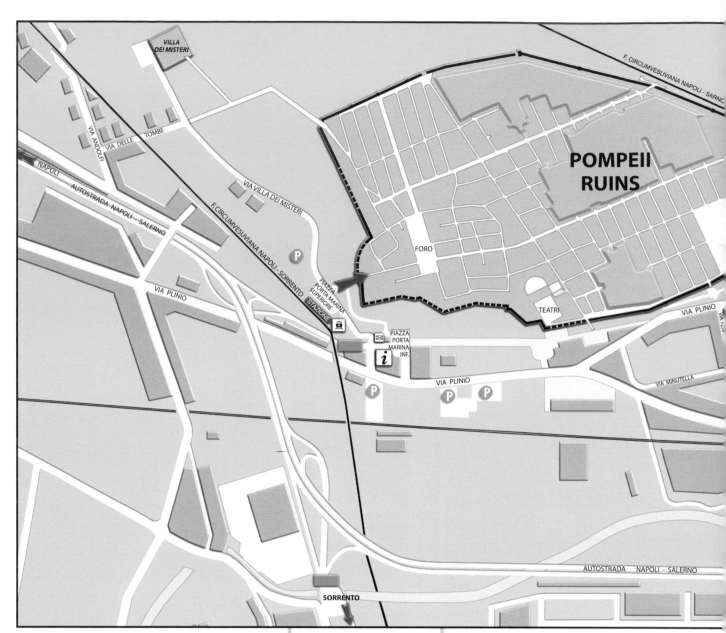

USEFUL TELEPHONE NUMBERS

Local Tourist Board,		
Offices Via Sacra 1		850.72.55
Free Phone	167	01.33.50
Information: Piazza Porta Marina Inf.		
State Police		850.61.72
Carabinieri		850.61.63
Municipal Police		850.61.64
First Aid		535.91.11
Doctor on-call		850.61.93
Canale Pharmacy		850.72.02
Del Rosario Pharmacy		850.73.33
Verdura Pharmacy		863.10.44
Town Hall		850.60.00
Archaeological Superintendent's Office		861.10.51
The Shrine to the Madonna of Pompeii		850.70.00
State Railways		850.61.76
Circumvesuviana Railway		779.21.11
Capodichino Airport		789.62.03
Banks - Bureaux de Change		
Banco Ambrosiano Veneto		850.21.19
Banca Popolare dell'Irpinia		850.80.33
Banco di Napoli		863.10.01
Banca di Roma		863.45.36
Banca di Credito Cooperativo		850.69.27
Monte dei Paschi di Siena		850.25.00

How to reach the archaeological site:

- Two bus routes offering a frequent service link the town centre to the Villa of Mysteries with numerous stops in-between.
- The Colourful horse-drawn carriages link the Porta Marina Gate to the Villa of the Mysteries and the centre of the modern town. We advise tourists to agree on the tariff with the driver before beginning their trip.
- We advise motorists to park their vehicles in one of the numerous authorised car parks.
- For further information and the latest timetables, please contact the local tourist authority offices at

PUBLIC TRANSPORT

MOUNT VESUVIUS

OPLONTIS
TORRE
ANNUNZIATA

NAPLES

ERCOLANO

PROCIDA
ISCHIA
CAPRI
SORRENTO

POMPE
VILLA OF MYSTERII

DISTANCES CHART

POMPEII - NAPLES	**km 20**
POMPEII - SALERNO	**km 25**
POMPEII - SORRENTO	**km 33**
POMPEII - POZZUOLI	**km 40**
POMPEII - ERCOLANO	**km 15**
POMPEII - MOUNT VESUVIUS	**km 30**
POMPEII - MOUNT FAITO	**km 35**
POMPEII - POSITANO	**km 45**
POMPEII - AMALFI	**km 60**
POMPEII - PAESTUM	**km 65**

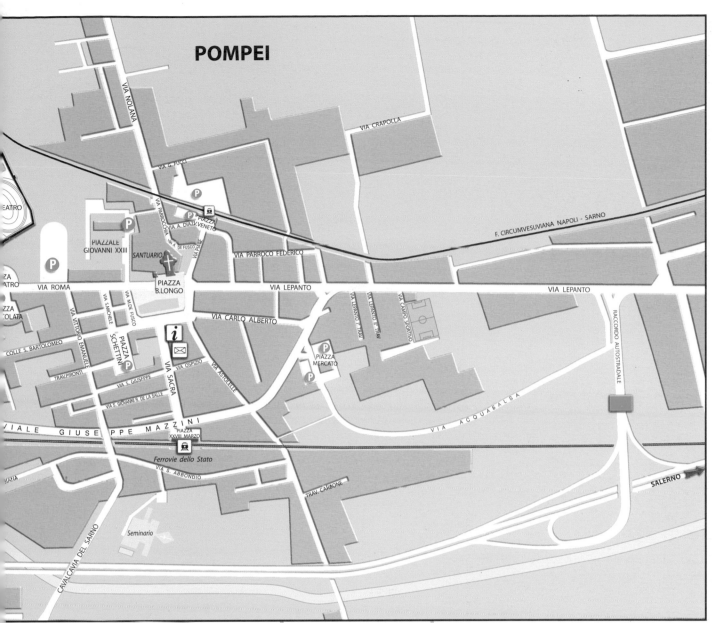

POMPEI

VIA NOLANA
VIA CRAPOLLA
VIA G. FUCCI
VIA PARROCCHIA
VIA A. DIAZ
VIA A. DE FUSCO
PIAZZA VENETO
PIAZZALE GIOVANNI XXIII
SANTUARIO
VIA PARROCO FEDERICO
F. CIRCUMVESUVIANA NAPOLI - SARNO
PIAZZA B.LONGO
VIA ROMA
VIA LEPANTO
VIA LEPANTO
VIA M.DE FUSCO
VIA S.MICHELE
VIA CARLO ALBERTO
VIA CAMPO SPORTIVO
VIA LEPANTO T. TRAV
VIA LEPANTO I TRAV
VIA VITTORIO EMANUELE
PIAZZA SCHETTINI
COLLE S. BARTOLOMEO
TRAV.PIRONTI
VIA S.GIUSEPPE
VIA SACRA
VIA OSPIZIO
VIA ASTOLELLE
PIAZZA MERCATO
RACCORDO AUTOSTRADALE
VIA S. GIOVANNI R. DE LA SALLE
VIA ACQUA SALSA
VIALE GIUSEPPE MAZZINI
PIAZZA XXVIII MARZO
Ferrovie dello Stato
VIA S. ABBONDIO
TRAV. CARBONE
SALERNO
CAVALCAVIA DEL SARNO
Seminario

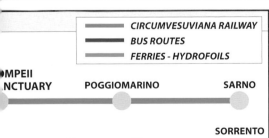

CIRCUMVESUVIANA RAILWAY
BUS ROUTES
FERRIES - HYDROFOILS

POMPEII SANCTUARY — POGGIOMARINO — SARNO

SORRENTO

CASTELLAMMARE DI STABIA
STABIAE
VICO EQUENSE
CAPRI

For trips and excursions to Naples, Herculaneum, Mount Vesuvius, Oplontis and the Sorrentine Peninsular, use the Circumvesuviana Railway. Many ferry and hydrofoil services run from Naples and Sorrento to the Islands in the Gulf of Naples: Capri, Ischia and Procida.

A frequent bus service with buses departing from Piazza Anfiteatro links Pompeii to the archaeological sites of Oplontis and Herculaneum and to Mount Vesuvius.

The large crowd applauds Frank Sinatra at his concert in the Large Theatre of the Pompeii archaeological site.

SHOWS

In summer, numerous shows and concerts are held in the theatres and the amphitheatre of Pompeii. Contact the local tourist board for further information.

Index of Buildings

Glossary

Amphora. Large terracotta container used predominantly for storing wine.

Apodyterium. Changing room in a Roman baths complex.

Apollo. God of the sun.

Apse. Room or area with a semicircular or polygonal plan.

Atrium. Main room in the house, used for receiving and entertaining guests.

Bacchus. God of wine.

Bucchero or **boccaro.** Black tinted ceramic work typical of Etruscan production between the 7th and the 5th centuries B.C.

Calidarium. The hottest room in a Roman baths complex where customers could take a hot bath.

Caupona. An inn or tavern.

Cavea. The terraced seating for the public inside Roman theatres.

Centaurs. Mythological figures with a human torso on a horse's body.

Cherub. A winged mythological figure: the offspring of Bacchus and Venus.

Cinnabar. A flame red colour obtained from mercury.

Compluvium. An opening in the ceiling of the atrium to allow light into the house and to collect rain water in a tank on the floor, called the impluvium, of the same size as the compluvium and positioned exactly below it.

Cryptoporticus. A porch or gallery, one or more sides of which are below ground level.

Cubiculum. A bed-chamber, generally small in size.

Decumanus. A main street in a Roman town, running east-west and intersecting with the various cardines which run north-south. This rational street plan was the development of the layout of military camps; in Pompeii the decumanus is Via dell'Abbondanza.

Diaeta. Dining room.

Exedra. A room with seats arranged in a semicircle for relaxation and conversation.

Fresco. A wall painting technique in which the paint is applied directly onto the plaster before it dries.

Frigidarium. A room in a Roman baths complex where customers could take a cold bath.

Hypocaustum. A heating system in which hot air was made to circulate through the cavities deliberately made in walls and floors.

Insula. A housing block formed by the intersection of north-south and east-west streets.

Isis. An Egyptian goddess.

Lanista. Someone who owns, rents or trains gladiators.

Lararium. A small shrine containing the Lares or tutelary gods of the house or district.

Mars. God of war.

Mosaic. A technique for making designs and pictures by juxtaposing small stone blocks or tiles.

Oecus. A room for receptions and celebrations.

Pappamonte. Blackish tufa-stone material obtained from volcanic ashes.

Peristyle. An inner courtyard surrounded by a colonnade with an arcade onto which numerous rooms in the house opened out.

Poppaea. The wife of the Emperor Nero. She owned a superb villa at Oplontis.

Praefurnium. A fire place for heating the Roman baths.

Pumice. Very light and porous stones erupted by the volcano.

Satyrs. Mythological figures from the court of Dionysus.

Sestertius. A Roman coin minted originally in silver but later in bronze.

Sudatorium. A room in a Roman baths complex similar to a modern-day sauna.

Suspensurae. Small brick columns supporting a floor. They were used to create a cavity beneath the floor for heating purposes (see Hypocaustum).

Taberna. A shop.

Tablinum. A room in a Roman house between the atrium and the peristyle which was used as a sort of office for the household business. This was where the tabulae, or accounts and other documents, were kept.

Tepidarium. A room in a Roman baths complex where customers could take a warm bath.

Tetrastyle. A building, room or area with four columns.

Thermopolium. Restaurant-inn. These had no real kitchen up until the 1st century B.C. as certain regulations regarding law and order tried to restrict sales to just wine.

Titus. The Emperor reigning at the time of the eruption. He succeeded his father Titus Flavius Vespasianus.

Triclinium. Dining room where members of the household and guests could eat a meal reclining on couches.

Venationes. Shows involving armed combat or wild animal hunts, held in the Amphitheatre.

Vestibulum. An entrance hall.